# If found, please return to:

name _____

phone _____

email _____

*Thank you.*

# We Donate 10% of Revenue* to Charity

*  Yes, that's 10% of *revenue*, not profits.

For example, if we sell $100 of books, and charge $5
for shipping to Canada (U.S. shipping is free),
and collect $7 in sales tax, we'll donate
$10 to charity (10% of the $100 sale).

As you see, we don't count shipping or sales
tax towards the 10% charity donation.

Money will go to a different charitable cause every month.

**These will often be 501(c)(3) nonprofits, but <u>not</u> <u>always</u>.**

We're making this pledge in good faith, hoping
to donate a lot of money every month, forever.

If this donation policy turns out to be unsustainable and
we decide to change, we will communicate that
clearly *before* actually making any change.

Learn more at streakersjournal.com

# STREAKER'S JOURNAL

by Mark Gavagan

streakersjournal.com

 @streakersj

Published by Cole House LLC
2 Tempe Wick Road, #91
Mendham, NJ 07945  USA

For inquiries about sales in **bulk quantities**, including corporate/premium sales, or **live presentations/seminars**, please contact the publisher at Cole House LLC, 2 Tempe Wick Road, #91 Mendham, NJ 07945  USA or www.colehouse.net

# Contents

# Thank You, Influencers

This journal has taken shape over several decades of reading, classes, videos, live presentations, and countless experiences.

Right now, I can't possibly remember & thank every person who's influenced my knowledge and thinking, but here's a partial listing:

Eric D. Thomas
Stephen Covey
Tony Robbins
Mel Robbins
Clay Christensen
Seth Godin
Charles Duhigg
Inky Johnson
Tim Ferriss
Ryan Carson
Dale Carnegie
Bernard Roth
Dave Martin
Bill Burnett
Dave Evans
Jason Wang
Paul Wendler
Catherine Hoke
Thomas Oppong
Derek Sivers
Ben Arment
Bruce Van Horn

Jason Fried
Nir Eyal
Ryan Holiday
Steven Levy
Neville Medhora
Benjamin P. Hardy
Warren Buffett
James Clear
Brad Feld
David Kadavy
Chase Jarvis
J. Allen Seinfeld
Vince Tizzio
Ralph Desantis
David Hansson
Michael Hyatt
Gail Winfrey
A.M. Slaughter
Gabriel Weinberg
Jeff Harmon
Michael Connell
Colin & Kelly Harris

Greg McKeown
F & J Wilson
Matt & Donna Gavagan
A & M Chernoff
A. Schwarzenegger
Zig Ziglar
Patricia Mackey
Frank Hawkinson
Armand Mastraccio
Simon Sinek
Brendon Burchard
Malcolm Gladwell
Gary Vaynerchuk
Brené Brown
Richard Branson
William Blanchfield
Jim Rohn
Phillip McGraw
Chris Guillebeau
Amy Hoy
Chris Voss

And last, but certainly not least, I would like to thank my lovely and endlessly patient wife and editor-in-chief, Kimberly.

# Why "Streaker's" Journal?

The idea is that every time you do the things you set out to do for at least three days in a row, we say that you're "on a streak."

If you're on a streak, you are a "streaker."

Hopefully these streaks will happen **a lot**, because it's a clear sign of effort and progress. Be proud of it!

*When someone asks how you're doing
or what you've been up to, just say
"I'm streaking!"*

# Why a Separate Book?

The first hundred drafts of this journal had thirty-plus workbook-style pages to help readers identify where they are right now (what's working well, and what isn't) and where they want to go (goals, dreams, habits, etc.).

I learned through user feedback that having all this in the beginning of a 9 week journal isn't the best idea. Here's why:

- All those pages add bulk and weight, making the journal less portable (and kind of overwhelming).

- After 9 weeks, you'll have a new journal, but many of the same goals. You'll have learned a lot and made lots of progress, but going through the *entire* discovery and documentation process for all your goals probably won't be necessary.

Visit **streakersjournal.com** to learn more about finding direction and setting meaningful goals, via blog posts, videos, suggested books, and my own, in-depth workbook.

# Why Only 9 Weeks?

This journal covers nine weeks, or a bit over two months.

I intended to have each journal cover three months (four journals per year), but realized either it would be way too large (it's already 270 pages) or I'd have to cut the number of pages for each week.

I tried *endless* variations and finally decided that the current number of pages for each week is the least there could be, while still preserving the journal's value and integrity.

# How This Book is Structured

The front of the book includes the table of contents, short primers on a few key concepts, instructions, and then a section to help you write down your goals and sort out what steps to focus on during the next nine weeks.

Each week has the following 24 pages:

- "Plan for Next Week" section (4 pages)

- Two side-by-side pages, for each day of the week (14 pages), including spaces for planning each day ("Plan for Tomorrow") and reviewing it afterward ("Day in Review")

- "Last Week in Review" section (6 pages)

In the back are blank pages, with either lines or dot-grids, for additional notes, writing, ideas, artwork, etc.

# * IMPORTANT DIRECTIONS *

**How It Works**:

- Once you've worked out your goals (pp. 18-30) and what you want to focus on and accomplish over the next nine weeks (pp. 30-33), fill-in the first "Plan for Next Week" section (pp. 34-37).

- Next, the evening *before* Day 1, fill-in the first "Plan for Tomorrow" (p. 38, on the left side of the day's two-page "spread"). Focus here on what you'll do in the next 24 hours.

- The next morning, **at the very beginning of the day** you just planned, invest one minute to look through your plans and goals, so you know exactly what's important and what you need to do.

- Optional: As you accomplish things throughout your day, mark them "done" by checking the corresponding box. It feels *great*!

- At the end of the day, use the "Day in Review" (p. 39, on the right side of that day's spread) to quickly review how it went.

- Repeat! Turn the page and start the next "Plan for Tomorrow."

Once you get going, the daily and weekly cycles flow easily: review the day or week you just completed, then plan for the next one, and then execute your plan.

**Key Goals & Habits.** Each day's "Plan for Tomorrow" page (sample below) has this section. It's a core element, worth explaining.

There are five preset items: food, drink, exercise, relationships & focus*.

*"Focus" has <u>two</u> meanings here (use either or both):
(1) avoiding distractions
(2) listening very carefully

Write the specific action you're planning to take that day, for each one. E.g., "Focus: No social media or news, from 8am - 6pm."

# "Plan for Tomorrow" Instructions

When you complete an item, mark it as "Done"

Make sure these are your most important priorities for the day.

Circle boxes of items NOT done by end of the day

Easy way to track progress during the day

Spaces to add three other goals or habits for the day.

This helps you track when & how much you sleep. Feel free to skip it if you don't want to focus on it right now.

**Plan for Tomorrow**₁     Date: Tuesday ___Feb 2___

Three **Most Important** Things To Do: *(do them ASAP)*    Done

1. *Buy streakersjournal.com domain name*    ☒

2. *Finish writing Nobel Prize acceptance speech*    ☒

3. *Buy 500 copies of "Streaker's Journal" as gifts for friends, family, employees, strangers, etc.*    ⬜

**Key goals & habits** for tomorrow:    Done

• Food: *No sugar. 5 servings of vegetables Ø Ø Ø Ø Ø*    ☒

• Drink: *1 coffee. 8 glasses of water Ø Ø Ø Ø Ø Ø O O*    ⬜

• Exercise: *Stretch 5 minutes, 50 pushups, 2 mile walk*    ☒

• Relationships: *Call Mom tonight (focus & listen!)*    ☒

• Focus: *Only check & respond to email 10am & 4pm*    ☒

• *ZERO social media between 8am - 7pm*    ☒

• *Eye contact + FULL attention in every conversation*    ☒

• *Practice guitar for 20+ minutes*    ☒

I'm *grateful* for: *(Note: Don't just write something here. Pause for a few seconds, force yourself to physically smile, take a slow deep breath, and think of what you're **truly** grateful for)*

| SLEEP | In bed | Devices off | Asleep by | Awake at | # sleep hours |
|---|---|---|---|---|---|
| Plan | 9:00pm | 9:15 | 10:00 | 5:03 | 7 hours |
| Actual | 9:30pm | 9:30 | 10:30 | 5:04 | 6.5 hours |

If you check every "Done" box for an entire day, that's a "Clean Sweep" (bravo!). Draw a vertical line through all the boxes (optional).

**Blank "Key Goals & Habits" spaces.** Beneath the five preset items are three blank spaces, each beginning with a bullet point.

These blank spaces are <u>NOT</u> intended for your "to-do" list of errands. One option for those is to put them in the "write or draw anything" section, on the bottom of the opposite page.

Use the blank spaces for things that are *important* to you and can help you make progress, even if they seem minor. Remember, **momentum matters and small things add up over time**.

Ideally some of these will be related to habits you want to track and develop, so you'll eventually do them on autopilot.

All of your "Key goals and habits" can be identical from one day to the next, or completely different. Whatever helps *you* is just fine.

Flossing your teeth is a terrific example of an item to put in one of the four blank spaces (unless you already floss every day).

It's specific, provides great benefits, can obviously be done within a single day, and it's easy to measure whether you did it or not.

Scroll down a few pages to the "Choosing Goals" section to learn more.

These spaces can also be filled with things you intend to avoid, such as social media, watching television during the week, etc.

Large or small, just make sure to fill-in all eight items *every* day. If you're stuck, "smile and say hello to someone" works great!

**Checking "Done" Boxes.** Throughout the day, as you finish them, (or at the end of each day, if you prefer), check off the "done" boxes on the right side of the "Plan for Tomorrow" page.

**Clean Sweep.** If you check all of the "Done" boxes for a single day, this is called a "Clean Sweep."

Feel free to draw a vertical line through them, signifying your victory!

**Morning Look.** Make sure to quickly look through each day's plan very early in your day. This will orient you towards what matters.

# Other Instructions

Once you finish a "Day in Review" or "Last Week in Review," take what you can from it and move-on by literally turning the page to the next planning page.

**Quick.** This journal should usually take only a few minutes in the morning and evening. Be thoughtful *and* quick, so you'll stay with it.

Feel free to abbreviate, write incomplete sentences, sketch rough pictures, etc. Whatever clearly conveys your thought is fine.

HOWEVER, make sure what you write today will be *legible* and *make sense* when you look back on it in 3 weeks or 3 years.

**Blank spaces are 100% fine.** If you're stuck on an item and don't have anything to say about it that day, just leave that space blank.

Also, once you've given it a chance, if you decide that keeping track of your "# of incoming streak days" from week to week on your "Streaking'" page (opposite page) isn't helpful, feel free to skip it.

**Skipping days.** You might decide to skip an entire day in your journal, or maybe even take weekends or vacations off. It's up to you and perfectly fine either way.

However, instead of automatically skipping your journal on vacations, for example, consider using it to help you focus on getting everything you want out of your vacation time.

"Vacation goals" might include tons of extra sleep, strengthening relationships, staying away from email and social media, "smelling the flowers," making sure to have dessert every night, etc..

When you've earned it, consider posting one of our <u>free</u>
**"I'm Streaking"** badges on your blog or social media:

### streakersjounrnal.com/badges

# "Streaking" Instructions

Ideally these pages will have lots of X's & arrows!

Mark ( X ) each circle ( ○ ) if the item was "Done" on the corresponding day that week.

This refers to the # of days in a row an item was "Done" exiting the prior week.

Next week's incoming # of streak days for Food would be 2 (Sat & Sun).

These refer to the spaces to add three other goals or habits for the day.

Every item "done" for a day is a "Clean Sweep" (awesome!)

And now some fun: **Streaking!**

Mark the circle for each item "done" on the corresponding day:

| # of incoming streak days | Mon | Tues | Wed | Thurs | Fri | Sat | Sun |
|---|---|---|---|---|---|---|---|
| Wrote in Journal ⑫ | X | X | X | X | X | X | X ► |
| Important #1 | X | ○ | ○ | ○ | ○ | ○ | ○ |
| Important #2    4 | X | X | X | ○ | ○ | ○ | ○ |
| Important #3 | X | ○ | ○ | ○ | ○ | ○ | ○ |
| Food | X | ○ | ○ | ○ | ○ | ► X | X ► |
| Drink | X | ○ | ○ | ○ | ○ | ○ | ○ |
| Exercise ⑩ | X | X | X | X | X | X | X ► |
| Relationships | X | ○ | ○ | ○ | ○ | ○ | ○ |
| Focus | X | ○ | ○ | ○ | ○ | ○ | ○ |
| *(1st blank item)* | X | ○ | ○ | ○ | ○ | ○ | ○ |
| *(2nd blank item)* | X | ○ | ○ | ○ | ○ | ○ | ○ |
| *(3rd blank item)* | X | ○ | ○ | ○ | ○ | ○ | ○ |

This streak ended at 7

Every time you have at least 3 boxes in a row or all the boxes in a column checked, draw a vertical or horizontal line through them.

* Three days in a row of checked circles, even if some are from last week, means **YOU ARE STREAKING!**

* If every box in *one* entire row is checked, you are on a **POWER STREAK!** Awesome!

* If *every* box, in *every* row, is checked, you are on a **MONSTER STREAK!** Congratulations! You are Incredible!

Drawing an arrow shows you have "done" an item at least one day heading into next week, so you'll have a number to enter in next week's "# of incoming streak days." Exercise would be 17 (10 + 7).

# The Long Term = Many Short Terms

Think about what you want your life to look like a year from now.

It seems like a long time, but those 52 weeks can zip right by.

**Here's what 1 year looks like** (each circle represents a day):

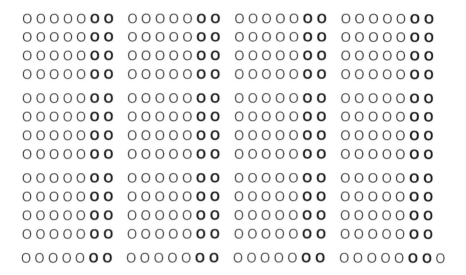

## *All of these days are going to pass, so*

# *Make Them Count!*

   * Pick objectives that matter to you

   * Learn what to do & how to do it

   * Use your time well (don't waste it)

# Habits Determine Your Life

A habit or routine is something you do regularly.

As Charles Duhigg explains in his insightful book, *The Power of Habit*\*, once something becomes a habit, it's difficult to change.

*\* terrific overview of the book, by Derek Sivers: http://bit.ly/habit-book*

Habits are powerful. They *become* our default behavior (autopilot).

Unless you consciously *choose* to consider alternatives, your brain just operates on autopilot and steers you towards your habits.

And doing the same thing over and over again, for a long period of time, can have *huge* consequences.

Think of how, over time, a stream of water cut through thousands of feet of rock to form the Grand Canyon.

*Get in the **habit** of winning by consistently doing a few easy, positive things, every single day*

That's why it's so powerful and important to curb bad habits and develop good ones - the effects add-up over time.

In other words, **positive habits help you constantly move forward, on autopilot, without even really trying**.

**Three parts to any habit** (Charles Duhigg's "habit loop"):

1. <u>cue</u> - triggers the brain to automatically begin the routine

2. <u>routine</u> - a physical, mental or emotional act

3. <u>reward</u> - some feeling or outcome the brain desires (even if it's not necessarily good for you), after the routine

Example: Every morning, I read my *Streaker's Journal* written goal to drink a giant glass of water when I wake up (cue); I drink water from the same giant glass (routine); and I feel refreshed, proud & satisfied as I check that item's "done" box in my journal (reward).

# Change A Habit

*Instead of "breaking" a bad habit, you're more likely to succeed\* if you try to transform it into a better one.*

~ Charles Duhigg

*\* Read Duhigg's explanation & story of how he lost weight by changing his daily chocolate chip cookie habit at:* **www.bit.ly/habits-101**

**To transform a habit**, you need to figure out its trigger (cue) and reward, and then find a new behavior that satisfies both.

Cues usually fall into one of five categories: time, location, people, emotion or ritual.

Duhigg believes any habit can be diagnosed and shifted, but you need to give yourself time to figure out the cues and rewards that are driving that behavior (often through trial and error).

Duhigg's short video on habit-breaking: **www.bit.ly/habit-vid** .

## Moderation vs. Always / Never

Most things are okay in moderation (smaller amounts, not consumed too often).

For example, while on paper it might be better to never have some unhealthy food you just love, it will be very difficult to completely banish that delicious food and never have it again.

Also, life is meant to be enjoyed.

Obviously, there are cases where abstinence is the only path to success, but often, instead of clenching your fists and trying to *never* eat that food again, consider having a *small* serving once or twice a week, instead of a giant serving every day.

# Simple Win / Low-Hanging Fruit

What is one free and simple thing you could do *every* day for the next 9 weeks, that would make your life better?

- ☐ Free
- ☐ Simple
- ☐ Easy to do every day
- ☐ Not a painful effort or sacrifice
- ☐ Makes your life better (right away or over time)
- ☐ Improves your life in a way that's important to you

_____

_____

_____

Benefits - How would your life become better?

_____

_____

It might be something like:

- putting your keys in a specific place every time you come home, so you never have to search for them again; or

- switching your 10am drink from cola to water, saving you money and calories; or

- asking a loved one a question every day and *really* listening to the answer, so your relationship gets stronger.

**It's up to you, but consider making whatever you wrote above one of your "Key goals & habits," that you do every day.**

**Brainstorm** as many ideas* as you can for "key goals & habits" or other goals you *might* pursue (decide later), related to each item:

Food: _____

_____

_____

_____

Drink: _____

_____

_____

_____

Exercise: _____

_____

_____

_____

Relationships: _____

_____

_____

_____

Focus: _____

_____

_____

_____

*What do you want to start, change, improve or continue?*

**Continue brainstorming** additional ideas for "key goals & habits," better sleep, or other goals you *might* pursue (decide later).

Refer back to the *"Where are you now?"* topics from page 18, including work, school, health, relationships, mental & emotional health, personal finances, volunteering, recreation, getting enough sleep, learning, organization, commute, living arrangements, etc..

_____

_____

_____

_____

_____

_____

_____

_____

_____

_____

_____

_____

_____

_____

_____

_____

_____

# On Relationships

You can't control how other people feel or behave. All you can control is **you.** Be interested in the other person, listen attentively, be helpful, kind, respectful, trustworthy, forgiving & understanding.

Also, consider whether you owe someone an apology. If you do, make it sincere, specific, and without any excuses or expectations. *Learn more: http://bit.ly/apology-101*

Sometimes, even if you do everything above, the chemistry, timing or history between people just doesn't work. It's also possible a relationship has run its course, or is just not fulfilling for one or both people.

> ***It's better to be alone than with someone who doesn't appreciate you and treat you well.***

Also, we rarely know all the things another person is dealing with, both past and present.

One of Steven Covey's *Seven Habits of Highly Successful People* is to first truly understand the *other* person, *then* seek to be understood.

This means listening fully and carefully (put down your phone). It's fine to ask questions and make sure you understand, but don't argue or debate.

Once you've listened, consider what the other person has said, and *then* respectfully share your point of view.

Lastly, **avoid unhealthy and abusive relationships.** If you or someone else are in a dangerous situation, or need someone to talk to, or you are an abuser, contact the non-profit **National Domestic Violence Hotline** (*confidential* help & advice):

- phone: 1-800-799-7233
- text (TTY): 1-800-787-3224
- web: www.thehotline.org

# Goals: What Do You Want?

What do you want? It's a simple question, but incredibly difficult for most people to answer.

This journal barely scratches the surface of this question, because it's primarily a tool for planning, execution and accountability on the steps you need to take every day and week.

Visit **streakersjournal.com** to learn more about finding direction and setting meaningful goals, via blog posts, videos, suggested books, and my own workbooks, tools & free resources.

**Where Are You Now?** Bill Burnett & Dave Evans, authors of the terrific book, *Designing Your Life*, advocate an idea rooted in design theory:

*Before identifying where you want to go (goals),*

*figure out where you are right now*

In other words, (1) deeply consider all aspects of your current life, including work, school, health, relationships, mental & emotional health, personal finances, volunteering, recreation, getting enough sleep, learning, organization, commute, living arrangements, etc., and then (2) figure out what's working well and bringing you happiness, progress or satisfaction, and what isn't.

You probably already have some ideas, but make sure you think carefully and really understand the root causes behind things that are and aren't going well.

Consider investing some time to write about everything above in the blank pages at the back of this journal, or elsewhere.

# SMART Goals

Wikipedia credits Peter Drucker for the concept that George Duran later coined as "SMART" goal-setting criteria.

There are many interpretations of what each letter of "SMART" stands for today, but the one below works well:

**S**pecific – Clearly defined, so you know exactly where the finish line is.

**M**easurable – You can to measure or quantify whether progress is being made. It's helpful to create simple metrics that reveal progress.

**A**ctionable – You can do things that affect whether or not progress gets made. An extension of this is how you'll do it (steps you'll take, resources you'll need, etc.).

**R**elevant – Why it's meaningful to you (motivation).

**T**ime-bound – Has a set deadline for completion.

Here's an example, created by Michael Hyatt, of a goal that's not SMART:  "I want to lose some weight." It's really just a vague desire.

Here's a SMART version of that goal: "I want to lose 8 pounds, over the next 2 months, so I'll have more energy at work and feel more confident at the beach. I'll start drinking water instead of soda and walk for 20 minutes every weekday, during lunch."

Let's see how it meets the SMART criteria:

- **S**pecific - drop 8 pounds
- **M**easurable - use a scale to measure weight
- **A**ctionable - walk 20 minutes per day + switch to water
- **R**elevant - more energy & confidence
- **T**ime-bound - 2 months

# Avoid Goals That Aren't Meaningful *To You*

This may sound simple and obvious, but there's a great and often unconscious tendency to allow our deepest dreams and desires to get buried beneath the fears, limiting beliefs and expectations of others.

If everyone limited themselves to what other people thought was "realistic," there would be no human greatness.

It's helpful to try and figure out what's driving you towards something.

- Are the motivations behind your goal healthy for you?

- Are there better alternatives than your goal to meet those needs?

- Are you truly interested in a master's degree, or is this a socially acceptable way to avoid something or boost your self esteem?

- Do you really want to be an actor, or are you craving what you imagine* it's like to be famous?

   *Jenna Fischer's book,* The Actor's Life: A Survival Guide, *provides an insider's story of how difficult, uncertain & unglamorous an actor's life really is.*

I can't predict the future or what you might succeed at or find fulfilling, and neither can any of those other people in your life.

> *"Failure is painful, but rarely worse than the regret of not trying"*

Only <u>you</u> can judge what your motivations are and what's worth spending your life's precious few moments on. Think. Be brave.

# Choosing Goals

At some point, you need to make a decision and choose something, which of course means *not* choosing other things.

Thankfully, most choices are easy to change, without causing negative consequences.

While this can be good in one sense, because you're not permanently stuck with a bad decision, there's also the concern that a person might not stick with something long enough to endure the difficulties required in reaching any worthwhile goal.

Before quitting something, ask yourself whether you're quitting simply because it's difficult, or it's truly wrong or no longer interesting or worthwhile for you.

Part of the difficulty in choosing goals is that there's often a huge gap between what we *think* or imagine something is like and what it's *actually* like in real life.

For example, being a lawyer is usually nothing like the glamorous television show *L.A. Law*.

Unfortunately, thousands of people spent three years in law school + hundreds of thousands of tuition dollars to learn this.

Instead of making decisions based on guesses & assumptions, Bill Burnett & Dave Evans, authors of the A+ book *Designing Your Life,* suggest **quick, low-risk experiments** or investigations, to learn for yourself what something is *really* like.

## Growth

Keep in mind that you will grow & change, even over nine weeks.

Things that seemed difficult, worthwhile, or interesting may become easy habits, so it may be time to move on to something different or more challenging.

Or, you might simply lose interest and prefer something else.

# Right-Sizing (Don't Overdo It in the Short Term)

Because many people want to make lots of progress very quickly, there's a tendency to start out with steps that are *way* too difficult.

> *Ambitious goals are great, but taking an unrealistically difficult or unsustainable path to reach them isn't.*

Attempting too much too soon often results in quick frustration and failure.

Instead, Gary Vaynerchuk urges patience ("Don't rush the process").

> *The sweet spot for making real progress is pushing yourself hard, so you strain and stretch yourself, without overdoing it.*

For example, I might not be able to run at top speed from New York to Los Angeles tonight, but if I'm a little more patient and realistic, I can *definitely** walk there in a few months.

> *\* In fact, if anyone is willing to donate $5 million to a 501(c)(3) charity that genuinely helps people in need, as thanks, I will pay my own expenses and literally walk from New York to Los Angeles.*
>
> *Just to be clear, the entire $5 million will go directly to charity.*

**Be Flexible**. If you're overwhelmed or exhausted on a given day or week, consider changing some goals to other, positive things that will *help*, like stretching, prayer, meditation and more sleep.

If you're *consistently* overwhelmed and not accomplishing many of your goals, you may have to figure out what can be eliminated to make room in your life, or maybe rethink and adjust your goals.

# Long-Term Goals

Write down your *most important* long term (SMART) goals and explain why each goal is meaningful **to you** (purpose):

_____

_____

_____

_____

_____

_____

_____

_____

_____

_____

_____

_____

_____

_____

_____

_____

_____

_____

_____

_____

_____

_____

_____

_____

_____

_____

_____

_____

_____

_____

_____

_____

_____

_____

_____

**_Important_**: *It's perfectly fine if you don't yet have a crystal clear idea of exactly what you want to do with your life.*

*Instead of just "filling in the blank space" above with something you know isn't genuine, just be honest with yourself and (1) acknowledge that you don't yet know what your goals are; and (2) start the process of trying to figure some of them out.*

**In fact, if you don't already know them, figuring out your long-term goals is a terrific goal for the next 9 weeks!**

*Find help and resources at **streakersjournal.com***

# Break Long-Term Goals Down Into *Small* Steps

It might be daunting to think about some of your long term goals. Where do you start? How can you possibly achieve it?

Here's how:

1.  Break each goal down into small, manageable steps;

2.  Prioritize them, so they're in the right order; and then

3.  Execute (consistently, one step after another)

Break your long-term goals into small steps or milestones. Put them in the right order and circle or underline the ones you plan to accomplish over the next 9 weeks:

_____

_____

_____

_____

_____

_____

_____

_____

_____

_____

_____

_____

# Goals for the Next 9 Weeks

What would you like to be *different* about you or your life 9 weeks from now?

How can you make progress on your long-term (SMART) goals over the next 9 weeks (small steps or short-term milestones)?

What habits (pp. 15-19) would you like to work on developing, stopping or transforming?

_____

_____

_____

_____

_____

_____

_____

_____

_____

_____

_____

_____

_____

_____

_____

# 9 Week Breakdown

Now that you've identified what you want to do over the next 9 weeks, break it down into the **steps you need to take during each week**, in order to reach each goal:

**Week 1**: _____

_____

_____

_____

_____

_____

**Week 2**: _____

_____

_____

_____

_____

**Week 3**: _____

_____

_____

_____

_____

**Week 4**: _____

_____

_____

_____

_____

_____

_____

**Week 5**: _____

_____

_____

_____

_____

_____

**Week 6**: _____

_____

_____

_____

_____

_____

Plans are great, but you'll probably find that circumstances may change or you'll be ahead or behind during the next 9 weeks.

Adjust & improvise as needed, but **keep making progress!**

**Week 7:** _____

_____

_____

_____

_____

_____

**Week 8:** _____

_____

_____

_____

_____

_____

_____

**Week 9:** _____

_____

_____

_____

_____

_____

When you finish, apply whatever you wrote for week 1 above to Week 1's *Plan for Next Week* section (begins on the next page).

# Plan for <u>Next</u> Week [1]  _____ *thru* _____

What is the **_Most Critical Thing_** next week, over which you have at least *some* control? Why is it so important?

_____

_____

_____

With your *best* effort, is it *possible* for you to succeed?  ☐ No  ☐ Yes

What is the #1 thing *you* can do to ensure a successful outcome?

_____

_____

_____

What else must you do to prepare and execute most effectively? Be specific. Outline *when* and *how* you will do each of them.

_____

_____

_____

_____

_____

_____

_____

_____

_____

What are you happy or excited about this week?

_____

_____

_____

What's likely to be difficult this week? How can you best handle it?

_____

_____

_____

What's one thing you can do this week to *simplify* or streamline your life, so you can focus more on what really matters?

_____

_____

_____

What do you need to do during *the next seven days* to make meaningful progress towards your **long-term goals**?

_____

_____

_____

What *key goal or habit* do you want to focus on this week? How?

_____

_____

_____

# Plan for Next Week

<u>**7 Day Calendar + Notes**</u>      ( *schedule your priorities <u>first</u>* )

Monday  _____   _____
         *(date)*
_____

_____

_____

_____

_____

Tuesday  _____   _____
          *(date)*
_____

_____

_____

_____

_____

Wednesday  _____   _____
            *(date)*
_____

_____

_____

_____

_____

Thursday _____ _____
             *(date)*

_____

_____

_____

_____

Friday _____ _____
           *(date)*

_____

_____

_____

_____

Saturday _____ _____
             *(date)*

_____

_____

_____

_____

Sunday _____ _____
            *(date)*

_____

_____

_____

# Plan for Tomorrow[1]

Date: Monday _____

Three **Most Important** Things To Do:   *(do them ASAP)*          *Done*

1. _____   ☐

_____

2. _____   ☐

_____

3. _____   ☐

_____

**Key goals & habits** for tomorrow:          *Done*

· Food: _____   ☐

· Drink: _____   ☐

· Exercise: _____   ☐

· Relationships: _____   ☐

· Focus: _____   ☐

· _____   ☐

· _____   ☐

· _____   ☐

I'm *grateful* for: _____

_____

_____

| SLEEP | In bed | Devices off | Asleep by | Awake at | # sleep hours |
|-------|--------|-------------|-----------|----------|---------------|
| Plan  |        |             |           |          |               |
| Actual|        |             |           |          |               |

On a scale of 1-10, how well did you use your time?     _____

What was fun or went well? When did you feel most engaged & alive?

_____

_____

_____

_____

What did you learn? What do you wish you did *better* or *differently*?

_____

_____

_____

_____

Any funny, sad or difficult moments? _____

_____

_____

_____

_____

Write or draw *anything*:

# Plan for Tomorrow₂

Date: Tuesday _____

Three **Most Important** Things To Do:  *(do them ASAP)*  *Done*

1. _____  ☐

   _____

2. _____  ☐

   _____

3. _____  ☐

   _____

**Key goals & habits** for tomorrow:  *Done*

· Food: _____  ☐

· Drink: _____  ☐

· Exercise: _____  ☐

· Relationships: _____  ☐

· Focus: _____  ☐

· _____  ☐

· _____  ☐

· _____  ☐

I'm *grateful* for: _____

_____

_____

| SLEEP | In bed | Devices off | Asleep by | Awake at | # sleep hours |
|-------|--------|-------------|-----------|----------|---------------|
| Plan |  |  |  |  |  |
| Actual |  |  |  |  |  |

On a scale of 1-10, how well did you use your time?   _____

What was fun or went well?  When did you feel most engaged & alive?

_____

_____

_____

_____

What did you learn? What do you wish you did *better* or *differently*?

_____

_____

_____

_____

Any funny, sad or difficult moments?  _____

_____

_____

_____

_____

Write or draw *anything*:

# Plan for Tomorrow[3]

Date: Wednesday _____

Three **Most Important** Things To Do:   *(do them ASAP)*                 *Done*

1. _____   ☐

   _____

2. _____   ☐

   _____

3. _____   ☐

   _____

**Key goals & habits** for tomorrow:                                        *Done*

· Food: _____   ☐

· Drink: _____   ☐

· Exercise: _____   ☐

· Relationships: _____   ☐

· Focus: _____   ☐

· _____   ☐

· _____   ☐

· _____   ☐

I'm *grateful* for: _____

_____

_____

| SLEEP | In bed | Devices off | Asleep by | Awake at | # sleep hours |
|-------|--------|-------------|-----------|----------|---------------|
| Plan   |        |             |           |          |               |
| Actual |        |             |           |          |               |

On a scale of 1-10, how well did you use your time? _____

What was fun or went well? When did you feel most engaged & alive?

_____

_____

_____

_____

What did you learn? What do you wish you did *better* or *differently*?

_____

_____

_____

_____

Any funny, sad or difficult moments? _____

_____

_____

_____

_____

Write or draw *anything*:

# Plan for Tomorrow₄

Date: Thursday _____

Three **Most Important** Things To Do:  *(do them ASAP)*          *Done*

1. _____  ☐

_____

2. _____  ☐

_____

3. _____  ☐

_____

**Key goals & habits** for tomorrow:                    *Done*

· Food: _____  ☐

· Drink: _____  ☐

· Exercise: _____  ☐

· Relationships: _____  ☐

· Focus: _____  ☐

· _____  ☐

· _____  ☐

· _____  ☐

I'm *grateful* for: _____

_____

_____

| SLEEP | In bed | Devices off | Asleep by | Awake at | # sleep hours |
|---|---|---|---|---|---|
| Plan | | | | | |
| Actual | | | | | |

On a scale of 1-10, how well did you use your time?  _____

What was fun or went well?  When did you feel most engaged & alive?

_____

_____

_____

_____

What did you learn?  What do you wish you did *better* or *differently*?

_____

_____

_____

_____

Any funny, sad or difficult moments?  _____

_____

_____

_____

Write or draw *anything*:

# Plan for Tomorrow₅

Date: Friday _____

Three **Most Important** Things To Do:   *(do them ASAP)*         *Done*

1. _____   ☐

   _____

2. _____   ☐

   _____

3. _____   ☐

   _____

**Key goals & habits** for tomorrow:                          *Done*

· Food: _____   ☐

· Drink: _____   ☐

· Exercise: _____   ☐

· Relationships: _____   ☐

· Focus: _____   ☐

· _____   ☐

· _____   ☐

· _____   ☐

I'm *grateful* for: _____

_____

_____

| SLEEP | In bed | Devices off | Asleep by | Awake at | # sleep hours |
|---|---|---|---|---|---|
| Plan | | | | | |
| Actual | | | | | |

On a scale of 1-10, how well did you use your time?  _____

What was fun or went well?  When did you feel most engaged & alive?

_____

_____

_____

_____

What did you learn? What do you wish you did *better* or *differently*?

_____

_____

_____

_____

Any funny, sad or difficult moments?  _____

_____

_____

_____

_____

Write or draw *anything*:

# Plan for Tomorrow[6]

Date:  Saturday  _____

Three **Most Important** Things To Do:   *(do them ASAP)*          *Done*

1. _____  ☐

   _____

2. _____  ☐

   _____

3. _____  ☐

   _____

## **Key goals & habits** for tomorrow:                    *Done*

· Food: _____  ☐

· Drink: _____  ☐

· Exercise: _____  ☐

· Relationships: _____  ☐

· Focus: _____  ☐

· _____  ☐

· _____  ☐

· _____  ☐

I'm *grateful* for: _____

_____

_____

| SLEEP | In bed | Devices off | Asleep by | Awake at | # sleep hours |
|-------|--------|-------------|-----------|----------|---------------|
| Plan   |        |             |           |          |               |
| Actual |        |             |           |          |               |

# Day in Review

On a scale of 1-10, how well did you use your time? _____

What was fun or went well? When did you feel most engaged & alive?

_____

_____

_____

_____

What did you learn? What do you wish you did *better* or *differently*?

_____

_____

_____

_____

Any funny, sad or difficult moments? _____

_____

_____

_____

_____

Write or draw *anything*:

# Plan for Tomorrow[7]

Date: Sunday _____

Three **Most Important** Things To Do:   *(do them ASAP)*          *Done*

1. _____  ☐

   _____

2. _____  ☐

   _____

3. _____  ☐

   _____

**Key goals & habits** for tomorrow:                    *Done*

· Food: _____  ☐

· Drink: _____  ☐

· Exercise: _____  ☐

· Relationships: _____  ☐

· Focus: _____  ☐

· _____  ☐

· _____  ☐

· _____  ☐

I'm *grateful* for: _____

_____

_____

| SLEEP | In bed | Devices off | Asleep by | Awake at | # sleep hours |
|-------|--------|-------------|-----------|----------|---------------|
| Plan  |        |             |           |          |               |
| Actual|        |             |           |          |               |

On a scale of 1-10, how well did you use your time?          _____

What was fun or went well?  When did you feel most engaged & alive?

_____

_____

_____

_____

What did you learn? What do you wish you did *better* or *differently*?

_____

_____

_____

_____

Any funny, sad or difficult moments?  _____

_____

_____

_____

_____

Write or draw *anything*:

Did you accomplish last week's **Most Critical Thing**?  ☐ No  ☐ Yes

Summarize what happened: _____

_____

_____

_____

_____

What did you do well? _____

_____

_____

_____

What do you wish you did differently? _____

_____

_____

_____

Were your *"I'm grateful for..."* responses thoughtful & heartfelt?

☐ Not really   ☐ Somewhat   ☐ Mostly   ☐ Definitely

How well did you use your *time*?   * *Enter your numbers from the top-right of each "Day in Review" page*

| Mon | Tues | Wed | Thurs | Fri | Sat | Sun | Total | Average |
|-----|------|-----|-------|-----|-----|-----|-------|---------|
|     |      |     |       |     |     |     |       |         |

Is your average *better, equal* or *worse* than the prior week? _____

Did you work on the *right things*, in the *right order*? If not, why?

_____

_____

_____

_____

Were you laser-*focused* or easily distracted? What were the worst *distractions* & time-wasters? How can you manage or avoid them?

_____

_____

_____

_____

Compare your *effort* last week to the very best you are capable of:

_____

_____

_____

_____

Was your overall *attitude* mostly positive and enthusiastic, or something else? How did that affect you?

_____

_____

_____

_____

And now some fun: **Streaking!**

Mark the circle for each item "done" on the corresponding day:

| # of incoming streak days | Mon | Tues | Wed | Thurs | Fri | Sat | Sun |
|---|---|---|---|---|---|---|---|
| Wrote in Journal | ○ | ○ | ○ | ○ | ○ | ○ | ○ |
| Important #1 | ○ | ○ | ○ | ○ | ○ | ○ | ○ |
| Important #2 | ○ | ○ | ○ | ○ | ○ | ○ | ○ |
| Important #3 | ○ | ○ | ○ | ○ | ○ | ○ | ○ |
| Food | ○ | ○ | ○ | ○ | ○ | ○ | ○ |
| Drink | ○ | ○ | ○ | ○ | ○ | ○ | ○ |
| Exercise | ○ | ○ | ○ | ○ | ○ | ○ | ○ |
| Relationships | ○ | ○ | ○ | ○ | ○ | ○ | ○ |
| Focus | ○ | ○ | ○ | ○ | ○ | ○ | ○ |
| *(1st blank item)* | ○ | ○ | ○ | ○ | ○ | ○ | ○ |
| *(2nd blank item)* | ○ | ○ | ○ | ○ | ○ | ○ | ○ |
| *(3rd blank item)* | ○ | ○ | ○ | ○ | ○ | ○ | ○ |

Every time you have at least 3 boxes in a row or all the boxes in a column checked, draw a vertical or horizontal line through them.

* Three days in a row of checked circles, even if some are from last week, means **YOU ARE STREAKING!**

* If every box in *one* entire row is checked, you are on a **POWER STREAK!** Awesome!

* If *every* box, in *every* row, is checked, you are on a **MONSTER STREAK!** Congratulations! You are Incredible!

Did you make meaningful progress towards your **long-term** goals last week? How can next week be better?

_____

_____

_____

How do you feel about your direction & progress for each item below? What changes should you make next week?

Food / Drink: _____

_____

_____

Exercise: _____

_____

_____

Relationships: _____

_____

_____

Focus: _____

_____

_____

Sleep: _____

*Enter your actual # of sleep hours from last week:*

| Sun | Mon | Tues | Wed | Thurs | Fri | Sat | Total | Average |
|-----|-----|------|-----|-------|-----|-----|-------|---------|
|     |     |      |     |       |     |     |       |         |

Notes, ideas, **and** how you feel about your direction & progress for **other things*** you focused on last week:

_____

_____

_____

_____

_____

_____

_____

_____

_____

_____

_____

_____

_____

_____

_____

_____

_____

_____

*\* Such as work, school, personal finances, meditation, prayer, reading, learning, long-term goals, mental health, dental habits, volunteering, etc.*

_____

_____

_____

_____

_____

_____

_____

_____

_____

_____

The *Plan for Next Week* section has a hidden gem: "What's one thing you can do this week to simplify or streamline your life?"

This means eliminating or minimizing things, people and activities that aren't satisfying or worthwhile **to you**, so you can make room for things that are.

Learn more via Greg McKeown's terrific book *Essentialism*.

# Plan for **<u>Next</u> Week** <sub>2</sub> _____ *thru* _____

What is the **Most Critical Thing** next week, over which you have at least *some* control? Why is it so important?

_____

_____

_____

With your *best* effort, is it *possible* for you to succeed?  ☐ No  ☐ Yes

What is the #1 thing *you* can do to ensure a successful outcome?

_____

_____

_____

What else must you do to prepare and execute most effectively? Be specific. Outline *when* and *how* you will do each of them.

_____

_____

_____

_____

_____

_____

_____

_____

What are you happy or excited about this week?

_____

_____

_____

What's likely to be difficult this week? How can you best handle it?

_____

_____

_____

What bold relationship risk *could* you take next week (stranger, friend, colleague, spouse, etc.)? What's the worst thing that could happen? What's the best?

_____

_____

_____

What do you need to do during *the next seven days* to make meaningful progress towards your **long-term goals**?

_____

_____

_____

What *key goal or habit* do you want to focus on this week? How?

_____

_____

_____

# Plan for Next Week

## 7 Day Calendar + Notes     ( *schedule your priorities __first__* )

Monday _____  _____
        *(date)*

_____

_____

_____

_____

_____

Tuesday _____  _____
         *(date)*

_____

_____

_____

_____

_____

Wednesday _____  _____
           *(date)*

_____

_____

_____

_____

_____

Thursday _____ _____
*(date)*

_____

_____

_____

_____

Friday _____ _____
*(date)*

_____

_____

_____

_____

Saturday _____ _____
*(date)*

_____

_____

_____

_____

Sunday _____ _____
*(date)*

_____

_____

_____

# Plan for Tomorrow[1]

Date: Monday _____

Three **Most Important** Things To Do: *(do them ASAP)*      *Done*

1. _____ ☐

 _____

2. _____ ☐

 _____

3. _____ ☐

 _____

**Key goals & habits** for tomorrow:      *Done*

· Food: _____ ☐

· Drink: _____ ☐

· Exercise: _____ ☐

· Relationships: _____ ☐

· Focus: _____ ☐

· _____ ☐

· _____ ☐

· _____ ☐

I'm *grateful* for: _____

_____

_____

| SLEEP | In bed | Devices off | Asleep by | Awake at | # sleep hours |
|---|---|---|---|---|---|
| Plan | | | | | |
| Actual | | | | | |

# Day in Review

On a scale of 1-10, how well did you use your time? _____

What was fun or went well? When did you feel most engaged & alive?

_____

_____

_____

_____

What did you learn? What do you wish you did *better* or *differently*?

_____

_____

_____

_____

Any funny, sad or difficult moments? _____

_____

_____

_____

_____

Write or draw *anything*:

# Plan for Tomorrow₂

Date: Tuesday _____

Three **Most Important** Things To Do:  *(do them ASAP)*     *Done*

1. _____  ☐

_____

2. _____  ☐

_____

3. _____  ☐

_____

**Key goals & habits** for tomorrow:     *Done*

· Food: _____  ☐

· Drink: _____  ☐

· Exercise: _____  ☐

· Relationships: _____  ☐

· Focus: _____  ☐

· _____  ☐

· _____  ☐

· _____  ☐

I'm *grateful* for: _____

_____

_____

| SLEEP | In bed | Devices off | Asleep by | Awake at | # sleep hours |
|---|---|---|---|---|---|
| Plan | | | | | |
| Actual | | | | | |

On a scale of 1-10, how well did you use your time?  _____

What was fun or went well?  When did you feel most engaged & alive?

_____

_____

_____

_____

What did you learn? What do you wish you did *better* or *differently*?

_____

_____

_____

_____

Any funny, sad or difficult moments?  _____

_____

_____

_____

_____

Write or draw *anything*:

# Plan for Tomorrow₃

Date: Wednesday _____

Three **Most Important** Things To Do:   *(do them ASAP)*        *Done*

1. _____   ☐

   _____

2. _____   ☐

   _____

3. _____   ☐

   _____

**Key goals & habits** for tomorrow:                          *Done*

· Food: _____   ☐

· Drink: _____   ☐

· Exercise: _____   ☐

· Relationships: _____   ☐

· Focus: _____   ☐

· _____   ☐

· _____   ☐

· _____   ☐

I'm *grateful* for: _____

_____

_____

| SLEEP | In bed | Devices off | Asleep by | Awake at | # sleep hours |
|---|---|---|---|---|---|
| Plan | | | | | |
| Actual | | | | | |

On a scale of 1-10, how well did you use your time?  _____

What was fun or went well?  When did you feel most engaged & alive?

_____

_____

_____

_____

What did you learn? What do you wish you did *better* or *differently*?

_____

_____

_____

_____

Any funny, sad or difficult moments?  _____

_____

_____

_____

_____

Write or draw *anything*:

# Plan for Tomorrow[4]

Date:  Thursday _____

Three **Most Important** Things To Do:   *(do them ASAP)*          *Done*

1. _____   ☐

   _____

2. _____   ☐

   _____

3. _____   ☐

   _____


**Key goals & habits** for tomorrow:                              *Done*

· Food: _____   ☐

· Drink: _____   ☐

· Exercise: _____   ☐

· Relationships: _____   ☐

· Focus: _____   ☐

· _____   ☐

· _____   ☐

· _____   ☐

I'm *grateful* for: _____

_____

_____

| SLEEP | In bed | Devices off | Asleep by | Awake at | # sleep hours |
|---|---|---|---|---|---|
| Plan | | | | | |
| Actual | | | | | |

On a scale of 1-10, how well did you use your time?  _____

What was fun or went well?  When did you feel most engaged & alive?

_____

_____

_____

_____

What did you learn? What do you wish you did *better* or *differently*?

_____

_____

_____

_____

Any funny, sad or difficult moments?  _____

_____

_____

_____

_____

Write or draw *anything*:

# Plan for Tomorrow₅

Date: Friday _____

Three **Most Important** Things To Do:   *(do them ASAP)*               Done

1. _____ ☐

_____

2. _____ ☐

_____

3. _____ ☐

_____

**Key goals & habits** for tomorrow:                                    *Done*

· Food: _____ ☐

· Drink: _____ ☐

· Exercise: _____ ☐

· Relationships: _____ ☐

· Focus: _____ ☐

· _____ ☐

· _____ ☐

· _____ ☐

I'm *grateful* for: _____

_____

_____

| SLEEP | In bed | Devices off | Asleep by | Awake at | # sleep hours |
|---|---|---|---|---|---|
| Plan | | | | | |
| Actual | | | | | |

On a scale of 1-10, how well did you use your time? _____

What was fun or went well? When did you feel most engaged & alive?

_____

_____

_____

_____

What did you learn? What do you wish you did *better* or *differently*?

_____

_____

_____

_____

Any funny, sad or difficult moments? _____

_____

_____

_____

Write or draw *anything*:

# Plan for Tomorrow<sub>6</sub>

Date: Saturday _____

Three **Most Important** Things To Do:  *(do them ASAP)*                     *Done*

1. _____  ☐

   _____

2. _____  ☐

   _____

3. _____  ☐

   _____

**Key goals & habits** for tomorrow:                                        *Done*

· Food: _____  ☐

· Drink: _____  ☐

· Exercise: _____  ☐

· Relationships: _____  ☐

· Focus: _____  ☐

· _____  ☐

· _____  ☐

· _____  ☐

I'm *grateful* for: _____

_____

_____

| SLEEP | In bed | Devices off | Asleep by | Awake at | # sleep hours |
|-------|--------|-------------|-----------|----------|---------------|
| Plan   |        |             |           |          |               |
| Actual |        |             |           |          |               |

On a scale of 1-10, how well did you use your time? _____

What was fun or went well? When did you feel most engaged & alive?

_____

_____

_____

_____

What did you learn? What do you wish you did *better* or *differently*?

_____

_____

_____

_____

Any funny, sad or difficult moments? _____

_____

_____

_____

_____

Write or draw *anything*:

# Plan for Tomorrow[7]

Date: Sunday _____

Three **Most Important** Things To Do: *(do them ASAP)*     *Done*

1. _____ ☐

    _____

2. _____ ☐

    _____

3. _____ ☐

    _____

**Key goals & habits** for tomorrow:     *Done*

· Food: _____ ☐

· Drink: _____ ☐

· Exercise: _____ ☐

· Relationships: _____ ☐

· Focus: _____ ☐

· _____ ☐

· _____ ☐

· _____ ☐

I'm *grateful* for: _____

_____

_____

| SLEEP | In bed | Devices off | Asleep by | Awake at | # sleep hours |
|---|---|---|---|---|---|
| Plan | | | | | |
| Actual | | | | | |

On a scale of 1-10, how well did you use your time? _____

What was fun or went well?  When did you feel most engaged & alive?

_____

_____

_____

_____

What did you learn? What do you wish you did _better_ or _differently_?

_____

_____

_____

_____

Any funny, sad or difficult moments? _____

_____

_____

_____

Write or draw _anything_:

Did you accomplish last week's ***Most Critical Thing***? ☐ No ☐ Yes

Summarize what happened: _____

_____

_____

_____

_____

What did you do well? _____

_____

_____

_____

What do you wish you did differently? _____

_____

_____

_____

Were your *"I'm grateful for..."* responses thoughtful & heartfelt?

☐ Not really  ☐ Somewhat  ☐ Mostly  ☐ Definitely

How well did you use your *time*? *(top-right, "Day in Review" pages)*

| Mon | Tues | Wed | Thurs | Fri | Sat | Sun | Total | Average |
|-----|------|-----|-------|-----|-----|-----|-------|---------|
|     |      |     |       |     |     |     |       |         |

Is your average *better, equal* or *worse* than the prior week? _____

Did you work on the *right things*, in the *right order*? If not, why?

_____

_____

_____

_____

Were you laser-*focused* or easily distracted? What were the worst *distractions* & time-wasters? How can you manage or avoid them?

_____

_____

_____

_____

Compare your *effort* last week to the very best you are capable of:

_____

_____

_____

_____

Was your overall *attitude* mostly positive and enthusiastic, or something else? How did that affect you?

_____

_____

_____

_____

And now some fun:  # Streaking!

Mark the circle for each item "done" on the corresponding day:

| # of incoming streak days | Mon | Tues | Wed | Thurs | Fri | Sat | Sun |
|---|---|---|---|---|---|---|---|
| Wrote in Journal | ○ | ○ | ○ | ○ | ○ | ○ | ○ |
| Important #1 | ○ | ○ | ○ | ○ | ○ | ○ | ○ |
| Important #2 | ○ | ○ | ○ | ○ | ○ | ○ | ○ |
| Important #3 | ○ | ○ | ○ | ○ | ○ | ○ | ○ |
| Food | ○ | ○ | ○ | ○ | ○ | ○ | ○ |
| Drink | ○ | ○ | ○ | ○ | ○ | ○ | ○ |
| Exercise | ○ | ○ | ○ | ○ | ○ | ○ | ○ |
| Relationships | ○ | ○ | ○ | ○ | ○ | ○ | ○ |
| Focus | ○ | ○ | ○ | ○ | ○ | ○ | ○ |
| (1st blank item) | ○ | ○ | ○ | ○ | ○ | ○ | ○ |
| (2nd blank item) | ○ | ○ | ○ | ○ | ○ | ○ | ○ |
| (3rd blank item) | ○ | ○ | ○ | ○ | ○ | ○ | ○ |

Every time you have at least 3 boxes in a row or all the boxes in a column checked, draw a vertical or horizontal line through them.

* Three days in a row of checked circles, even if some are from last week, means **YOU ARE <u>STREAKING!</u>**

* If every box in *one* entire row is checked, you are on a **POWER STREAK!** Awesome!

* If *every* box, in *every* row, is checked, you are on a **<u>MONSTER</u> STREAK!** Congratulations! You are Incredible!

Did you make meaningful progress towards your **long-term** goals last week? How can next week be better?

_____

_____

_____

How do you feel about your direction & progress for each item below? What changes should you make next week?

Food/Drink: _____

_____

_____

Exercise: _____

_____

_____

Relationships: _____

_____

_____

Focus: _____

_____

_____

Sleep: _____

*Enter your actual # of sleep hours from last week:*

| Sun | Mon | Tues | Wed | Thurs | Fri | Sat | Total | Average |
|-----|-----|------|-----|-------|-----|-----|-------|---------|
|     |     |      |     |       |     |     |       |         |

Notes, ideas, **and** how you feel about your direction & progress for **other things*** you focused on last week:

_____

_____

_____

_____

_____

_____

_____

_____

_____

_____

_____

_____

_____

_____

_____

_____

_____

_____

*Such as work, school, personal finances, meditation, prayer, reading, learning, long-term goals, mental health, dental habits, volunteering, etc.*

# Plan for <u>Next</u> Week ₃ _____ *thru* _____

What is the **_Most Critical Thing_** next week, over which you have at least *some* control? Why is it so important?

_____

_____

_____

With your *best* effort, is it *possible* for you to succeed?  ☐ No  ☐ Yes

What is the #1 thing *you* can do to ensure a successful outcome?

_____

_____

_____

What else must you do to prepare and execute most effectively? Be specific. Outline *when* and *how* you will do each of them.

_____

_____

_____

_____

_____

_____

_____

_____

_____

What are you happy or excited about this week?

_____

_____

_____

What's likely to be difficult this week? How can you best handle it?

_____

_____

_____

What one specific thing could you put extra effort into this week that might impact your success or happiness?

_____

_____

_____

What do you need to do during *the next seven days* to make meaningful progress towards your **long-term goals**?

_____

_____

_____

What *key goal or habit* do you want to focus on this week? How?

_____

_____

_____

## 7 Day Calendar + Notes          *( schedule your priorities **first** )*

Monday _____  _____
*(date)*

_____

_____

_____

_____

_____


Tuesday _____  _____
*(date)*

_____

_____

_____

_____

_____


Wednesday _____  _____
*(date)*

_____

_____

_____

_____

_____

Thursday _____ _____
<br>*(date)*

_____

_____

_____

_____

Friday _____ _____
<br>*(date)*

_____

_____

_____

_____

Saturday _____ _____
<br>*(date)*

_____

_____

_____

_____

Sunday _____ _____
<br>*(date)*

_____

_____

_____

# Plan for Tomorrow[1]

Date: Monday _____

Three **Most Important** Things To Do:   *(do them ASAP)*      *Done*

1. _____   ☐

   _____

2. _____   ☐

   _____

3. _____   ☐

   _____

**Key goals & habits** for tomorrow:                        *Done*

· Food: _____   ☐

· Drink: _____   ☐

· Exercise: _____   ☐

· Relationships: _____   ☐

· Focus: _____   ☐

· _____   ☐

· _____   ☐

· _____   ☐

I'm *grateful* for: _____

_____

_____

| SLEEP | In bed | Devices off | Asleep by | Awake at | # sleep hours |
|---|---|---|---|---|---|
| Plan | | | | | |
| Actual | | | | | |

On a scale of 1-10, how well did you use your time? _____

What was fun or went well? When did you feel most engaged & alive?

_____

_____

_____

_____

What did you learn? What do you wish you did *better* or *differently*?

_____

_____

_____

_____

Any funny, sad or difficult moments? _____

_____

_____

_____

_____

Write or draw *anything*:

# Plan for Tomorrow₂

Date: Tuesday _____

Three **Most Important** Things To Do:   *(do them ASAP)*                      *Done*

1. _____  ☐

   _____

2. _____  ☐

   _____

3. _____  ☐

   _____

**Key goals & habits** for tomorrow:                                          *Done*

· Food: _____  ☐

· Drink: _____  ☐

· Exercise: _____  ☐

· Relationships: _____  ☐

· Focus: _____  ☐

· _____  ☐

· _____  ☐

· _____  ☐

I'm *grateful* for: _____

_____

_____

| SLEEP | In bed | Devices off | Asleep by | Awake at | # sleep hours |
|---|---|---|---|---|---|
| Plan | | | | | |
| Actual | | | | | |

On a scale of 1-10, how well did you use your time? _____

What was fun or went well?  When did you feel most engaged & alive?

_____

_____

_____

_____

What did you learn? What do you wish you did *better* or *differently*?

_____

_____

_____

_____

Any funny, sad or difficult moments? _____

_____

_____

_____

_____

Write or draw *anything*:

# Plan for Tomorrow₃

Date: Wednesday _____

Three **Most Important** Things To Do:   *(do them ASAP)*   *Done*

1. _____ ☐

_____

2. _____ ☐

_____

3. _____ ☐

_____

**Key goals & habits** for tomorrow:   *Done*

· Food: _____ ☐

· Drink: _____ ☐

· Exercise: _____ ☐

· Relationships: _____ ☐

· Focus: _____ ☐

· _____ ☐

· _____ ☐

· _____ ☐

I'm *grateful* for: _____

_____

_____

| SLEEP | In bed | Devices off | Asleep by | Awake at | # sleep hours |
|---|---|---|---|---|---|
| Plan | | | | | |
| Actual | | | | | |

On a scale of 1-10, how well did you use your time? _____

What was fun or went well? When did you feel most engaged & alive?

_____

_____

_____

_____

What did you learn? What do you wish you did *better* or *differently*?

_____

_____

_____

_____

Any funny, sad or difficult moments? _____

_____

_____

_____

_____

Write or draw *anything*:

# Plan for Tomorrow[4]

Date: Thursday _____

Three **Most Important** Things To Do:  *(do them ASAP)*     *Done*

1. _____  ☐

_____

2. _____  ☐

_____

3. _____  ☐

_____

**Key goals & habits** for tomorrow:     *Done*

· Food: _____  ☐

· Drink: _____  ☐

· Exercise: _____  ☐

· Relationships: _____  ☐

· Focus: _____  ☐

· _____  ☐

· _____  ☐

· _____  ☐

I'm *grateful* for: _____

_____

_____

| SLEEP | In bed | Devices off | Asleep by | Awake at | # sleep hours |
|---|---|---|---|---|---|
| Plan | | | | | |
| Actual | | | | | |

On a scale of 1-10, how well did you use your time? _____

What was fun or went well? When did you feel most engaged & alive?

_____

_____

_____

_____

What did you learn? What do you wish you did _better_ or _differently_?

_____

_____

_____

_____

Any funny, sad or difficult moments? _____

_____

_____

_____

_____

Write or draw _anything_:

# Plan for Tomorrow₅

Date: Friday _____

Three **Most Important** Things To Do:   *(do them ASAP)*                Done

1. _____   ☐

_____

2. _____   ☐

_____

3. _____   ☐

_____

**Key goals & habits** for tomorrow:                                   *Done*

· Food: _____   ☐

· Drink: _____   ☐

· Exercise: _____   ☐

· Relationships: _____   ☐

· Focus: _____   ☐

· _____   ☐

· _____   ☐

· _____   ☐

I'm *grateful* for: _____

_____

_____

| SLEEP | In bed | Devices off | Asleep by | Awake at | # sleep hours |
|-------|--------|-------------|-----------|----------|---------------|
| Plan  |        |             |           |          |               |
| Actual|        |             |           |          |               |

On a scale of 1-10, how well did you use your time?    _____

What was fun or went well?  When did you feel most engaged & alive?

_____

_____

_____

_____

What did you learn? What do you wish you did *better* or *differently*?

_____

_____

_____

_____

Any funny, sad or difficult moments?  _____

_____

_____

_____

Write or draw *anything*:

# Plan for Tomorrow[6]

Date: Saturday _____

Three **Most Important** Things To Do:  *(do them ASAP)*      *Done*

1. _____  ☐

   _____

2. _____  ☐

   _____

3. _____  ☐

   _____

**Key goals & habits** for tomorrow:      *Done*

- Food: _____  ☐
- Drink: _____  ☐
- Exercise: _____  ☐
- Relationships: _____  ☐
- Focus: _____  ☐
- _____  ☐
- _____  ☐
- _____  ☐

I'm *grateful* for: _____

_____

_____

| SLEEP | In bed | Devices off | Asleep by | Awake at | # sleep hours |
|-------|--------|-------------|-----------|----------|---------------|
| Plan |  |  |  |  |  |
| Actual |  |  |  |  |  |

On a scale of 1-10, how well did you use your time?  _____

What was fun or went well? When did you feel most engaged & alive?

_____

_____

_____

_____

What did you learn? What do you wish you did *better* or *differently*?

_____

_____

_____

_____

Any funny, sad or difficult moments?  _____

_____

_____

_____

_____

Write or draw *anything*:

# Plan for Tomorrow[7]

Date: Sunday _____

Three **Most Important** Things To Do:  *(do them ASAP)*     *Done*

1. _____  ☐

   _____

2. _____  ☐

   _____

3. _____  ☐

   _____

**Key goals & habits** for tomorrow:     *Done*

· Food: _____  ☐

· Drink: _____  ☐

· Exercise: _____  ☐

· Relationships: _____  ☐

· Focus: _____  ☐

· _____  ☐

· _____  ☐

· _____  ☐

I'm *grateful* for: _____

_____

_____

| SLEEP | In bed | Devices off | Asleep by | Awake at | # sleep hours |
|---|---|---|---|---|---|
| Plan | | | | | |
| Actual | | | | | |

On a scale of 1-10, how well did you use your time? _____

What was fun or went well?  When did you feel most engaged & alive?

_____

_____

_____

_____

What did you learn? What do you wish you did *better* or *differently*?

_____

_____

_____

_____

Any funny, sad or difficult moments? _____

_____

_____

_____

_____

Write or draw *anything*:

Did you accomplish last week's ***Most Critical Thing***? ☐ No ☐ Yes

Summarize what happened: _____
_____
_____
_____
_____

What did you do well? _____
_____
_____
_____

What do you wish you did differently? _____
_____
_____
_____

Were your *"I'm grateful for..."* responses thoughtful & heartfelt?

☐ Not really   ☐ Somewhat   ☐ Mostly   ☐ Definitely

How well did you use your *time*? *(top-right, "Day in Review" pages)*

| Mon | Tues | Wed | Thurs | Fri | Sat | Sun | Total | Average |
|-----|------|-----|-------|-----|-----|-----|-------|---------|
|     |      |     |       |     |     |     |       |         |

Is your average *better, equal* or *worse* than the prior week? _____

Did you work on the *right things*, in the *right order*? If not, why?

_____

_____

_____

_____

Were you laser-*focused* or easily distracted? What were the worst *distractions* & time-wasters? How can you manage or avoid them?

_____

_____

_____

_____

Compare your *effort* last week to the very best you are capable of:

_____

_____

_____

_____

Was your overall *attitude* mostly positive and enthusiastic, or something else? How did that affect you?

_____

_____

_____

_____

And now some fun: **Streaking!**

Mark the circle for each item "done" on the corresponding day:

| # of incoming streak days | Mon | Tues | Wed | Thurs | Fri | Sat | Sun |
| --- | --- | --- | --- | --- | --- | --- | --- |
| Wrote in Journal | ○ | ○ | ○ | ○ | ○ | ○ | ○ |
| Important #1 | ○ | ○ | ○ | ○ | ○ | ○ | ○ |
| Important #2 | ○ | ○ | ○ | ○ | ○ | ○ | ○ |
| Important #3 | ○ | ○ | ○ | ○ | ○ | ○ | ○ |
| Food | ○ | ○ | ○ | ○ | ○ | ○ | ○ |
| Drink | ○ | ○ | ○ | ○ | ○ | ○ | ○ |
| Exercise | ○ | ○ | ○ | ○ | ○ | ○ | ○ |
| Relationships | ○ | ○ | ○ | ○ | ○ | ○ | ○ |
| Focus | ○ | ○ | ○ | ○ | ○ | ○ | ○ |
| (1st blank item) | ○ | ○ | ○ | ○ | ○ | ○ | ○ |
| (2nd blank item) | ○ | ○ | ○ | ○ | ○ | ○ | ○ |
| (3rd blank item) | ○ | ○ | ○ | ○ | ○ | ○ | ○ |

Every time you have at least 3 boxes in a row or all the boxes in a column checked, draw a vertical or horizontal line through them.

* Three days in a row of checked circles, even if some are from last week, means **YOU ARE STREAKING!**

* If every box in *one* entire row is checked, you are on a **POWER STREAK!** Awesome!

* If *every* box, in *every* row, is checked, you are on a **MONSTER STREAK!** Congratulations! You are Incredible!

Did you make meaningful progress towards your **long-term** goals last week? How can next week be better?

_____

_____

_____

How do you feel about your direction & progress for each item below? What changes should you make next week?

Food / Drink: _____

_____

_____

Exercise: _____

_____

_____

Relationships: _____

_____

_____

Focus: _____

_____

_____

Sleep: _____

*Enter your actual # of sleep hours from last week:*

| Sun | Mon | Tues | Wed | Thurs | Fri | Sat | Total | Average |
|-----|-----|------|-----|-------|-----|-----|-------|---------|
|     |     |      |     |       |     |     |       |         |

Notes, ideas, **and** how you feel about your direction & progress for **other things*** you focused on last week:

_____

_____

_____

_____

_____

_____

_____

_____

_____

_____

_____

_____

_____

_____

_____

_____

*Such as work, school, personal finances, meditation, prayer, reading, learning, long-term goals, mental health, dental habits, volunteering, etc.*

# Plan for **Next** Week 4 _____ *thru* _____

What is the **Most Critical Thing** next week, over which you have at least *some* control? Why is it so important?

_____

_____

_____

With your *best* effort, is it *possible* for you to succeed?  ☐ No  ☐ Yes

What is the #1 thing *you* can do to ensure a successful outcome?

_____

_____

_____

What else must you do to prepare and execute most effectively? Be specific. Outline *when* and *how* you will do each of them.

_____

_____

_____

_____

_____

_____

_____

_____

_____

What are you happy or excited about this week?

_____

_____

_____

What's likely to be difficult this week? How can you best handle it?

_____

_____

_____

Who in your past or present life do you feel truly grateful for, but you haven't told them recently? Consider telling them *this week.*

_____

_____

_____

What do you need to do during *the next seven days* to make meaningful progress towards your **long-term goals**?

_____

_____

_____

What *key goal or habit* do you want to focus on this week? How?

_____

_____

_____

# Plan for Next Week <sub>4</sub> *(cont'd)*

## 7 Day Calendar + Notes          *( schedule your priorities **first** )*

Monday _____ _____
_(date)_

_____

_____

_____

_____

_____

Tuesday _____ _____
_(date)_

_____

_____

_____

_____

_____

Wednesday _____ _____
_(date)_

_____

_____

_____

_____

_____

# Plan for Next Week 4 *(cont'd)*

Thursday _____ _____
*(date)*

_____

_____

_____

_____

Friday _____ _____
*(date)*

_____

_____

_____

_____

Saturday _____ _____
*(date)*

_____

_____

_____

_____

Sunday _____ _____
*(date)*

_____

_____

_____

# Plan for Tomorrow[1]

Date: Monday _____

Three **Most Important** Things To Do:  *(do them ASAP)*          *Done*

1. _____  ☐

   _____

2. _____  ☐

   _____

3. _____  ☐

   _____

**Key goals & habits** for tomorrow:          *Done*

· Food: _____  ☐

· Drink: _____  ☐

· Exercise: _____  ☐

· Relationships: _____  ☐

· Focus: _____  ☐

· _____  ☐

· _____  ☐

· _____  ☐

I'm *grateful* for: _____

_____

_____

| SLEEP | In bed | Devices off | Asleep by | Awake at | # sleep hours |
|---|---|---|---|---|---|
| Plan | | | | | |
| Actual | | | | | |

On a scale of 1-10, how well did you use your time?  _____

What was fun or went well?  When did you feel most engaged & alive?

_____

_____

_____

_____

What did you learn? What do you wish you did *better* or *differently*?

_____

_____

_____

_____

Any funny, sad or difficult moments?  _____

_____

_____

_____

_____

Write or draw *anything*:

# Plan for Tomorrow₂

Date: Tuesday _____

Three **Most Important** Things To Do:   *(do them ASAP)*          *Done*

1. _____   ☐

   _____

2. _____   ☐

   _____

3. _____   ☐

   _____

**Key goals & habits** for tomorrow:          *Done*

· Food: _____   ☐

· Drink: _____   ☐

· Exercise: _____   ☐

· Relationships: _____   ☐

· Focus: _____   ☐

· _____   ☐

· _____   ☐

· _____   ☐

I'm *grateful* for: _____

_____

_____

| SLEEP | In bed | Devices off | Asleep by | Awake at | # sleep hours |
|-------|--------|-------------|-----------|----------|---------------|
| Plan |  |  |  |  |  |
| Actual |  |  |  |  |  |

On a scale of 1-10, how well did you use your time?  _____

What was fun or went well? When did you feel most engaged & alive?

_____

_____

_____

_____

What did you learn? What do you wish you did *better* or *differently*?

_____

_____

_____

_____

Any funny, sad or difficult moments?  _____

_____

_____

_____

_____

Write or draw *anything*:

# Plan for Tomorrow₃

Date: Wednesday _____

Three **Most Important** Things To Do:  *(do them ASAP)*          *Done*

1. _____  ☐

   _____

2. _____  ☐

   _____

3. _____  ☐

   _____

**Key goals & habits** for tomorrow:          *Done*

· Food: _____  ☐

· Drink: _____  ☐

· Exercise: _____  ☐

· Relationships: _____  ☐

· Focus: _____  ☐

· _____  ☐

· _____  ☐

· _____  ☐

I'm *grateful* for: _____

_____

_____

| SLEEP | In bed | Devices off | Asleep by | Awake at | # sleep hours |
|-------|--------|-------------|-----------|----------|---------------|
| Plan   |        |             |           |          |               |
| Actual |        |             |           |          |               |

# Day in Review

On a scale of 1-10, how well did you use your time?  _____

What was fun or went well? When did you feel most engaged & alive?

_____

_____

_____

_____

What did you learn? What do you wish you did *better* or *differently*?

_____

_____

_____

_____

Any funny, sad or difficult moments? _____

_____

_____

_____

Write or draw *anything*:

# Plan for Tomorrow[4]

Date: Thursday _____

Three **Most Important** Things To Do:  *(do them ASAP)*    *Done*

1. _____   ☐

   _____

2. _____   ☐

   _____

3. _____   ☐

   _____

## Key goals & habits for tomorrow:    *Done*

· Food: _____   ☐

· Drink: _____   ☐

· Exercise: _____   ☐

· Relationships: _____   ☐

· Focus: _____   ☐

· _____   ☐

· _____   ☐

· _____   ☐

I'm *grateful* for: _____

_____

_____

| SLEEP | In bed | Devices off | Asleep by | Awake at | # sleep hours |
|--------|--------|-------------|-----------|----------|---------------|
| Plan   |        |             |           |          |               |
| Actual |        |             |           |          |               |

# Day in Review

On a scale of 1-10, how well did you use your time?  _____

What was fun or went well?  When did you feel most engaged & alive?

_____

_____

_____

_____

What did you learn? What do you wish you did *better* or *differently*?

_____

_____

_____

_____

Any funny, sad or difficult moments?  _____

_____

_____

_____

_____

Write or draw *anything*:

# Plan for Tomorrow[5]

Date: Friday _____

Three **Most Important** Things To Do:  *(do them ASAP)*     *Done*

1. _____  ☐

  _____

2. _____  ☐

  _____

3. _____  ☐

  _____

**Key goals & habits** for tomorrow:     *Done*

· Food: _____  ☐

· Drink: _____  ☐

· Exercise: _____  ☐

· Relationships: _____  ☐

· Focus: _____  ☐

· _____  ☐

· _____  ☐

· _____  ☐

I'm *grateful* for: _____

_____

_____

| SLEEP | In bed | Devices off | Asleep by | Awake at | # sleep hours |
|---|---|---|---|---|---|
| Plan |  |  |  |  |  |
| Actual |  |  |  |  |  |

On a scale of 1-10, how well did you use your time?     _____

What was fun or went well? When did you feel most engaged & alive?

_____

_____

_____

_____

What did you learn? What do you wish you did *better* or *differently*?

_____

_____

_____

_____

Any funny, sad or difficult moments?  _____

_____

_____

_____

_____

Write or draw *anything*:

# Plan for Tomorrow[6]

Date: Saturday _____

Three **Most Important** Things To Do:  *(do them ASAP)*          *Done*

1. _____  ☐

_____

2. _____  ☐

_____

3. _____  ☐

_____

**Key goals & habits** for tomorrow:          *Done*

· Food: _____  ☐

· Drink: _____  ☐

· Exercise: _____  ☐

· Relationships: _____  ☐

· Focus: _____  ☐

· _____  ☐

· _____  ☐

· _____  ☐

I'm *grateful* for: _____

_____

_____

| SLEEP | In bed | Devices off | Asleep by | Awake at | # sleep hours |
|-------|--------|-------------|-----------|----------|---------------|
| Plan | | | | | |
| Actual | | | | | |

# Day in Review

On a scale of 1-10, how well did you use your time?  _____

What was fun or went well? When did you feel most engaged & alive?

_____

_____

_____

_____

What did you learn? What do you wish you did *better* or *differently*?

_____

_____

_____

_____

Any funny, sad or difficult moments?  _____

_____

_____

_____

_____

Write or draw *anything*:

# Plan for Tomorrow[7]

Date: Sunday _____

Three **Most Important** Things To Do:  *(do them ASAP)*          *Done*

1. _____ ☐

_____

2. _____ ☐

_____

3. _____ ☐

_____

## **Key goals & habits** for tomorrow:                    *Done*

· Food: _____ ☐

· Drink: _____ ☐

· Exercise: _____ ☐

· Relationships: _____ ☐

· Focus: _____ ☐

· _____ ☐

· _____ ☐

· _____ ☐

I'm *grateful* for: _____

_____

_____

| SLEEP | In bed | Devices off | Asleep by | Awake at | # sleep hours |
|---|---|---|---|---|---|
| Plan | | | | | |
| Actual | | | | | |

On a scale of 1-10, how well did you use your time? _____

What was fun or went well? When did you feel most engaged & alive?

_____

_____

_____

_____

What did you learn? What do you wish you did *better* or *differently*?

_____

_____

_____

_____

Any funny, sad or difficult moments? _____

_____

_____

_____

_____

Write or draw *anything*:

## Last Week in Review _____ *thru* _____

Did you accomplish last week's **Most Critical Thing**? ☐ No ☐ Yes

Summarize what happened: _____

_____

_____

_____

_____

What did you do well? _____

_____

_____

_____

What do you wish you did differently? _____

_____

_____

_____

Were your *"I'm grateful for..."* responses thoughtful & heartfelt?

☐ Not really ☐ Somewhat ☐ Mostly ☐ Definitely

How well did you use your *time*? *(top-right, "Day in Review" pages)*

| Mon | Tues | Wed | Thurs | Fri | Sat | Sun | Total | Average |
|-----|------|-----|-------|-----|-----|-----|-------|---------|
|     |      |     |       |     |     |     |       |         |

Is your average *better, equal* or *worse* than the prior week? _____

Did you work on the *right things*, in the *right order*? If not, why?

_____

_____

_____

_____

Were you laser-*focused* or easily distracted? What were the worst *distractions* & time-wasters? How can you manage or avoid them?

_____

_____

_____

_____

Compare your *effort* last week to the very best you are capable of:

_____

_____

_____

_____

Was your overall *attitude* mostly positive and enthusiastic, or something else? How did that affect you?

_____

_____

_____

_____

And now some fun: **Streaking!**

Mark the circle for each item "done" on the corresponding day:

| # of incoming streak days | Mon | Tues | Wed | Thurs | Fri | Sat | Sun |
|---|---|---|---|---|---|---|---|
| Wrote in Journal | ○ | ○ | ○ | ○ | ○ | ○ | ○ |
| Important #1 | ○ | ○ | ○ | ○ | ○ | ○ | ○ |
| Important #2 | ○ | ○ | ○ | ○ | ○ | ○ | ○ |
| Important #3 | ○ | ○ | ○ | ○ | ○ | ○ | ○ |
| Food | ○ | ○ | ○ | ○ | ○ | ○ | ○ |
| Drink | ○ | ○ | ○ | ○ | ○ | ○ | ○ |
| Exercise | ○ | ○ | ○ | ○ | ○ | ○ | ○ |
| Relationships | ○ | ○ | ○ | ○ | ○ | ○ | ○ |
| Focus | ○ | ○ | ○ | ○ | ○ | ○ | ○ |
| (1st blank item) | ○ | ○ | ○ | ○ | ○ | ○ | ○ |
| (2nd blank item) | ○ | ○ | ○ | ○ | ○ | ○ | ○ |
| (3rd blank item) | ○ | ○ | ○ | ○ | ○ | ○ | ○ |

Every time you have at least 3 boxes in a row or all the boxes in a column checked, draw a vertical or horizontal line through them.

* Three days in a row of checked circles, even if some are from last week, means **YOU ARE STREAKING!**

* If every box in *one* entire row is checked, you are on a **POWER STREAK!** Awesome!

* If *every* box, in *every* row, is checked, you are on a **MONSTER STREAK!** Congratulations! You are Incredible!

Did you make meaningful progress towards your **long-term** goals last week? How can next week be better?

_____

_____

_____

How do you feel about your direction & progress for each item below? What changes should you make next week?

Food / Drink: _____

_____

_____

Exercise: _____

_____

_____

Relationships: _____

_____

_____

Focus: _____

_____

_____

Sleep: _____

*Enter your actual # of sleep hours from last week:*

| Sun | Mon | Tues | Wed | Thurs | Fri | Sat | Total | Average |
|-----|-----|------|-----|-------|-----|-----|-------|---------|
|     |     |      |     |       |     |     |       |         |

Notes, ideas, **and** how you feel about your direction & progress for **other things*** you focused on last week:

_____

_____

_____

_____

_____

_____

_____

_____

_____

_____

_____

_____

_____

_____

_____

_____

_____

*\* Such as work, school, personal finances, meditation, prayer, reading, learning, long-term goals, mental health, dental habits, volunteering, etc.*

# Plan for <u>Next</u> Week <sub>5</sub> _____ *thru* _____

What is the **Most Critical Thing** next week, over which you have at least *some* control? Why is it so important?

_____

_____

_____

With your *best* effort, is it *possible* for you to succeed? ☐ No ☐ Yes

What is the #1 thing *you* can do to ensure a successful outcome?

_____

_____

_____

What else must you do to prepare and execute most effectively? Be specific. Outline *when* and *how* you will do each of them.

_____

_____

_____

_____

_____

_____

_____

_____

_____

What are you happy or excited about this week?

_____

_____

_____

What's likely to be difficult this week? How can you best handle it?

_____

_____

_____

Is there anything regarding your personal or family finances that you've been putting off? Consider doing it *this week.*

_____

_____

_____

What do you need to do during *the next seven days* to make meaningful progress towards your **long-term goals**?

_____

_____

_____

What *key goal or habit* do you want to focus on this week? How?

_____

_____

_____

# Plan for Next Week <sub>5</sub> *(cont'd)*

## <u>7 Day Calendar + Notes</u>   *( schedule your priorities <u>first</u> )*

Monday _____  _____
*(date)*

_____

_____

_____

_____

_____

Tuesday _____  _____
*(date)*

_____

_____

_____

_____

_____

Wednesday _____  _____
*(date)*

_____

_____

_____

_____

Thursday _____ _____
          *(date)*

_____

_____

_____

_____

Friday _____ _____
          *(date)*

_____

_____

_____

_____

Saturday _____ _____
          *(date)*

_____

_____

_____

_____

Sunday _____ _____
          *(date)*

_____

_____

_____

# Plan for Tomorrow[1]

Date: Monday _____

Three **Most Important** Things To Do:  *(do them ASAP)*     *Done*

1. _____  ☐

   _____

2. _____  ☐

   _____

3. _____  ☐

   _____

**Key goals & habits** for tomorrow:     *Done*

- Food: _____  ☐

- Drink: _____  ☐

- Exercise: _____  ☐

- Relationships: _____  ☐

- Focus: _____  ☐

- _____  ☐

- _____  ☐

- _____  ☐

I'm *grateful* for: _____

_____

_____

| SLEEP | In bed | Devices off | Asleep by | Awake at | # sleep hours |
|--------|--------|-------------|-----------|----------|---------------|
| Plan | | | | | |
| Actual | | | | | |

On a scale of 1-10, how well did you use your time? _____

What was fun or went well? When did you feel most engaged & alive?

_____

_____

_____

_____

What did you learn? What do you wish you did _better_ or _differently_?

_____

_____

_____

_____

Any funny, sad or difficult moments? _____

_____

_____

_____

Write or draw _anything_:

# Plan for Tomorrow₂

Date: Tuesday _____

Three **Most Important** Things To Do:  *(do them ASAP)*                    *Done*

1. _____  ☐

   _____

2. _____  ☐

   _____

3. _____  ☐

   _____

## Key goals & habits for tomorrow:

*Done*

· Food: _____  ☐

· Drink: _____  ☐

· Exercise: _____  ☐

· Relationships: _____  ☐

· Focus: _____  ☐

· _____  ☐

· _____  ☐

· _____  ☐

I'm *grateful* for: _____

_____

_____

| SLEEP | In bed | Devices off | Asleep by | Awake at | # sleep hours |
|-------|--------|-------------|-----------|----------|---------------|
| Plan  |        |             |           |          |               |
| Actual|        |             |           |          |               |

# Day in Review

On a scale of 1-10, how well did you use your time?  _____

What was fun or went well? When did you feel most engaged & alive?

_____

_____

_____

_____

What did you learn? What do you wish you did *better* or *differently*?

_____

_____

_____

_____

Any funny, sad or difficult moments?  _____

_____

_____

_____

_____

Write or draw *anything*:

# Plan for Tomorrow₃

Date: Wednesday _____

Three **Most Important** Things To Do:  *(do them ASAP)*     *Done*

1. _____  ☐

   _____

2. _____  ☐

   _____

3. _____  ☐

   _____

**Key goals & habits** for tomorrow:     *Done*

· Food: _____  ☐

· Drink: _____  ☐

· Exercise: _____  ☐

· Relationships: _____  ☐

· Focus: _____  ☐

· _____  ☐

· _____  ☐

· _____  ☐

I'm *grateful* for: _____

_____

_____

| SLEEP | In bed | Devices off | Asleep by | Awake at | # sleep hours |
|-------|--------|-------------|-----------|----------|---------------|
| Plan   |        |             |           |          |               |
| Actual |        |             |           |          |               |

On a scale of 1-10, how well did you use your time? _____

What was fun or went well? When did you feel most engaged & alive?

_____

_____

_____

_____

What did you learn? What do you wish you did *better* or *differently*?

_____

_____

_____

_____

Any funny, sad or difficult moments? _____

_____

_____

_____

_____

Write or draw *anything*:

# Plan for Tomorrow₄

Date: Thursday _____

Three **Most Important** Things To Do:   *(do them ASAP)*          Done

1. _____   ☐

   _____

2. _____   ☐

   _____

3. _____   ☐

   _____

**Key goals & habits** for tomorrow:                              Done

· Food: _____   ☐

· Drink: _____   ☐

· Exercise: _____   ☐

· Relationships: _____   ☐

· Focus: _____   ☐

· _____   ☐

· _____   ☐

· _____   ☐

I'm *grateful* for: _____

_____

_____

| SLEEP | In bed | Devices off | Asleep by | Awake at | # sleep hours |
|-------|--------|-------------|-----------|----------|---------------|
| Plan  |        |             |           |          |               |
| Actual|        |             |           |          |               |

On a scale of 1-10, how well did you use your time? _____

What was fun or went well? When did you feel most engaged & alive?

_____

_____

_____

_____

What did you learn? What do you wish you did *better* or *differently*?

_____

_____

_____

_____

Any funny, sad or difficult moments? _____

_____

_____

_____

_____

Write or draw *anything*:

# Plan for Tomorrow₅

Date: Friday _____

Three **Most Important** Things To Do:  *(do them ASAP)*     Done

1. _____  ☐

   _____

2. _____  ☐

   _____

3. _____  ☐

   _____

**Key goals & habits** for tomorrow:                    Done

· Food: _____  ☐

· Drink: _____  ☐

· Exercise: _____  ☐

· Relationships: _____  ☐

· Focus: _____  ☐

· _____  ☐

· _____  ☐

· _____  ☐

I'm *grateful* for: _____

_____

_____

| SLEEP | In bed | Devices off | Asleep by | Awake at | # sleep hours |
|-------|--------|-------------|-----------|----------|---------------|
| Plan  |        |             |           |          |               |
| Actual |       |             |           |          |               |

# Day in Review

On a scale of 1-10, how well did you use your time? _____

What was fun or went well? When did you feel most engaged & alive?

_____

_____

_____

_____

What did you learn? What do you wish you did *better* or *differently*?

_____

_____

_____

_____

Any funny, sad or difficult moments? _____

_____

_____

_____

_____

Write or draw *anything*:

# Plan for Tomorrow[6]

Date: Saturday _____

Three **Most Important** Things To Do: *(do them ASAP)*   *Done*

1. _____ ☐

_____

2. _____ ☐

_____

3. _____ ☐

_____

**Key goals & habits** for tomorrow:   *Done*

· Food: _____ ☐

· Drink: _____ ☐

· Exercise: _____ ☐

· Relationships: _____ ☐

· Focus: _____ ☐

· _____ ☐

· _____ ☐

· _____ ☐

I'm *grateful* for: _____

_____

_____

| SLEEP | In bed | Devices off | Asleep by | Awake at | # sleep hours |
|---|---|---|---|---|---|
| Plan | | | | | |
| Actual | | | | | |

On a scale of 1-10, how well did you use your time?  _____

What was fun or went well? When did you feel most engaged & alive?

_____

_____

_____

_____

What did you learn? What do you wish you did *better* or *differently*?

_____

_____

_____

_____

Any funny, sad or difficult moments?  _____

_____

_____

_____

_____

Write or draw *anything*:

# Plan for Tomorrow[7]

Date: Sunday _____

Three **Most Important** Things To Do:  *(do them ASAP)*   *Done*

1. _____  ☐

_____

2. _____  ☐

_____

3. _____  ☐

_____

**Key goals & habits** for tomorrow:   *Done*

· Food: _____  ☐

· Drink: _____  ☐

· Exercise: _____  ☐

· Relationships: _____  ☐

· Focus: _____  ☐

· _____  ☐

· _____  ☐

· _____  ☐

I'm *grateful* for: _____

_____

_____

| SLEEP | In bed | Devices off | Asleep by | Awake at | # sleep hours |
|-------|--------|-------------|-----------|----------|---------------|
| Plan  |        |             |           |          |               |
| Actual|        |             |           |          |               |

# Day in Review

On a scale of 1-10, how well did you use your time? _____

What was fun or went well? When did you feel most engaged & alive?

_____

_____

_____

_____

What did you learn? What do you wish you did *better* or *differently*?

_____

_____

_____

_____

Any funny, sad or difficult moments? _____

_____

_____

_____

_____

Write or draw *anything*:

Did you accomplish last week's **Most Critical Thing**? ☐ No ☐ Yes

Summarize what happened: _____

_____

_____

_____

_____

What did you do well? _____

_____

_____

What do you wish you did differently? _____

_____

_____

_____

Were your *"I'm grateful for..."* responses thoughtful & heartfelt?

☐ Not really   ☐ Somewhat   ☐ Mostly   ☐ Definitely

How well did you use your *time*? *(top-right, "Day in Review" pages)*

| Mon | Tues | Wed | Thurs | Fri | Sat | Sun | Total | Average |
|-----|------|-----|-------|-----|-----|-----|-------|---------|
|     |      |     |       |     |     |     |       |         |

Is your average *better, equal* or *worse* than the prior week? _____

Did you work on the *right things*, in the *right order*? If not, why?

_____

_____

_____

_____

Were you laser-*focused* or easily distracted? What were the worst *distractions* & time-wasters? How can you manage or avoid them?

_____

_____

_____

_____

Compare your *effort* last week to the very best you are capable of:

_____

_____

_____

_____

Was your overall *attitude* mostly positive and enthusiastic, or something else? How did that affect you?

_____

_____

_____

_____

And now some fun:     # Streaking!

Mark the circle for each item "done" on the corresponding day:

| # of incoming streak days | Mon | Tues | Wed | Thurs | Fri | Sat | Sun |
|---|---|---|---|---|---|---|---|
| Wrote in Journal | ○ | ○ | ○ | ○ | ○ | ○ | ○ |
| Important #1 | ○ | ○ | ○ | ○ | ○ | ○ | ○ |
| Important #2 | ○ | ○ | ○ | ○ | ○ | ○ | ○ |
| Important #3 | ○ | ○ | ○ | ○ | ○ | ○ | ○ |
| Food | ○ | ○ | ○ | ○ | ○ | ○ | ○ |
| Drink | ○ | ○ | ○ | ○ | ○ | ○ | ○ |
| Exercise | ○ | ○ | ○ | ○ | ○ | ○ | ○ |
| Relationships | ○ | ○ | ○ | ○ | ○ | ○ | ○ |
| Focus | ○ | ○ | ○ | ○ | ○ | ○ | ○ |
| (1st blank item) | ○ | ○ | ○ | ○ | ○ | ○ | ○ |
| (2nd blank item) | ○ | ○ | ○ | ○ | ○ | ○ | ○ |
| (3rd blank item) | ○ | ○ | ○ | ○ | ○ | ○ | ○ |

Every time you have at least 3 boxes in a row or all the boxes in a column checked, draw a vertical or horizontal line through them.

* Three days in a row of checked circles, even if some are from last week, means **YOU ARE STREAKING!**

* If every box in *one* entire row is checked, you are on a **POWER STREAK!** Awesome!

* If *every* box, in *every* row, is checked, you are on a **MONSTER STREAK!** Congratulations! You are Incredible!

Did you make meaningful progress towards your **long-term** goals last week? How can next week be better?

_____

_____

_____

How do you feel about your direction & progress for each item below? What changes should you make next week?

Food / Drink: _____

_____

_____

Exercise: _____

_____

_____

Relationships: _____

_____

_____

Focus: _____

_____

_____

Sleep: _____

*Enter your actual # of sleep hours from last week:*

| Sun | Mon | Tues | Wed | Thurs | Fri | Sat | Total | Average |
|-----|-----|------|-----|-------|-----|-----|-------|---------|
|     |     |      |     |       |     |     |       |         |

Notes, ideas, **and** how you feel about your direction & progress for **other things*** you focused on last week:

_____

_____

_____

_____

_____

_____

_____

_____

_____

_____

_____

_____

_____

_____

_____

_____

_____

*Such as work, school, personal finances, meditation, prayer, reading, learning, long-term goals, mental health, dental habits, volunteering, etc.*

## Plan for **<u>Next</u> Week** <sub>6</sub> _____ *thru* _____

What is the **_Most Critical Thing_** next week, over which you have at least *some* control? Why is it so important?

_____

_____

_____

With your *best* effort, is it *possible* for you to succeed? ☐ No ☐ Yes

What is the #1 thing *you* can do to ensure a successful outcome?

_____

_____

_____

What else must you do to prepare and execute most effectively? Be specific. Outline *when* and *how* you will do each of them.

_____

_____

_____

_____

_____

_____

_____

_____

_____

What are you happy or excited about this week?

_____

_____

_____

What's likely to be difficult this week? How can you best handle it?

_____

_____

_____

What's one thing you can do this week to *simplify* or streamline your life, so you can focus more on what really matters?

_____

_____

_____

What do you need to do during *the next seven days* to make meaningful progress towards your **long-term goals**?

_____

_____

_____

What *key goal or habit* do you want to focus on this week? How?

_____

_____

_____

## 7 Day Calendar + Notes     *( schedule your priorities **first** )*

Monday _____  *(date)* _____

_____

_____

_____

_____

_____

Tuesday _____  *(date)* _____

_____

_____

_____

_____

_____

Wednesday _____  *(date)* _____

_____

_____

_____

_____

_____

Thursday _____
   *(date)*

_____

_____

_____

_____

Friday _____
   *(date)*

_____

_____

_____

_____

Saturday _____
   *(date)*

_____

_____

_____

_____

Sunday _____
   *(date)*

_____

_____

_____

# Plan for Tomorrow[1]

Date: Monday _____

Three **Most Important** Things To Do: *(do them ASAP)*　　Done

1. _____ ☐

_____

2. _____ ☐

_____

3. _____ ☐

_____

## **Key goals & habits** for tomorrow:

*Done*

· Food: _____ ☐

· Drink: _____ ☐

· Exercise: _____ ☐

· Relationships: _____ ☐

· Focus: _____ ☐

· _____ ☐

· _____ ☐

· _____ ☐

I'm *grateful* for: _____

_____

_____

| SLEEP | In bed | Devices off | Asleep by | Awake at | # sleep hours |
|--------|--------|-------------|-----------|----------|---------------|
| Plan | | | | | |
| Actual | | | | | |

On a scale of 1-10, how well did you use your time?     _____

What was fun or went well?  When did you feel most engaged & alive?

_____

_____

_____

_____

What did you learn? What do you wish you did *better* or *differently*?

_____

_____

_____

_____

Any funny, sad or difficult moments?  _____

_____

_____

_____

_____

Write or draw *anything*:

# Plan for Tomorrow₂

Date: Tuesday _____

Three **Most Important** Things To Do:  *(do them ASAP)*  *Done*

1. _____  ☐

   _____

2. _____  ☐

   _____

3. _____  ☐

   _____

## Key goals & habits for tomorrow:

*Done*

· Food: _____  ☐

· Drink: _____  ☐

· Exercise: _____  ☐

· Relationships: _____  ☐

· Focus: _____  ☐

· _____  ☐

· _____  ☐

· _____  ☐

I'm *grateful* for: _____

_____

_____

| SLEEP | In bed | Devices off | Asleep by | Awake at | # sleep hours |
|-------|--------|-------------|-----------|----------|---------------|
| Plan   |        |             |           |          |               |
| Actual |        |             |           |          |               |

On a scale of 1-10, how well did you use your time?  _____

What was fun or went well?  When did you feel most engaged & alive?

_____

_____

_____

_____

What did you learn?  What do you wish you did *better* or *differently*?

_____

_____

_____

_____

Any funny, sad or difficult moments?  _____

_____

_____

_____

_____

Write or draw *anything*:

# Plan for Tomorrow[3]

Date: Wednesday _____

Three **Most Important** Things To Do:  *(do them ASAP)*        *Done*

1. _____  ☐

   _____

2. _____  ☐

   _____

3. _____  ☐

   _____

**Key goals & habits** for tomorrow:                    *Done*

· Food: _____  ☐

· Drink: _____  ☐

· Exercise: _____  ☐

· Relationships: _____  ☐

· Focus: _____  ☐

· _____  ☐

· _____  ☐

· _____  ☐

I'm *grateful* for: _____

_____

_____

| SLEEP | In bed | Devices off | Asleep by | Awake at | # sleep hours |
|-------|--------|-------------|-----------|----------|---------------|
| Plan |  |  |  |  |  |
| Actual |  |  |  |  |  |

# **Day in Review**

On a scale of 1-10, how well did you use your time?      _____

What was fun or went well? When did you feel most engaged & alive?

_____

_____

_____

_____

What did you learn? What do you wish you did _better_ or _differently_?

_____

_____

_____

_____

Any funny, sad or difficult moments? _____

_____

_____

_____

_____

Write or draw _anything_:

# Plan for Tomorrow[4]

Date: Thursday _____

Three **Most Important** Things To Do:   *(do them ASAP)*       *Done*

1. _____  ☐

_____

2. _____  ☐

_____

3. _____  ☐

_____

**Key goals & habits** for tomorrow:                *Done*

· Food: _____  ☐

· Drink: _____  ☐

· Exercise: _____  ☐

· Relationships: _____  ☐

· Focus: _____  ☐

· _____  ☐

· _____  ☐

· _____  ☐

I'm *grateful* for: _____

_____

_____

| SLEEP | In bed | Devices off | Asleep by | Awake at | # sleep hours |
|-------|--------|-------------|-----------|----------|---------------|
| Plan  |        |             |           |          |               |
| Actual|        |             |           |          |               |

On a scale of 1-10, how well did you use your time?     _____

What was fun or went well?  When did you feel most engaged & alive?

_____

_____

_____

_____

What did you learn? What do you wish you did *better* or *differently*?

_____

_____

_____

_____

Any funny, sad or difficult moments? _____

_____

_____

_____

_____

Write or draw *anything*:

# Plan for Tomorrow₅

Date: Friday _____

Three **Most Important** Things To Do:  *(do them ASAP)*    *Done*

1. _____  ☐

_____

2. _____  ☐

_____

3. _____  ☐

_____

**Key goals & habits** for tomorrow:    *Done*

· Food: _____  ☐

· Drink: _____  ☐

· Exercise: _____  ☐

· Relationships: _____  ☐

· Focus: _____  ☐

· _____  ☐

· _____  ☐

· _____  ☐

I'm *grateful* for: _____

_____

_____

| SLEEP | In bed | Devices off | Asleep by | Awake at | # sleep hours |
|-------|--------|-------------|-----------|----------|---------------|
| Plan |  |  |  |  |  |
| Actual |  |  |  |  |  |

On a scale of 1-10, how well did you use your time?          _____

What was fun or went well?  When did you feel most engaged & alive?

_____

_____

_____

_____

What did you learn? What do you wish you did _better_ or _differently_?

_____

_____

_____

_____

Any funny, sad or difficult moments?  _____

_____

_____

_____

Write or draw _anything_:

# Plan for Tomorrow[6]

Date: Saturday _____

Three **Most Important** Things To Do:  *(do them ASAP)*  *Done*

1. _____  ☐

   _____

2. _____  ☐

   _____

3. _____  ☐

   _____

**Key goals & habits** for tomorrow:  *Done*

· Food: _____  ☐

· Drink: _____  ☐

· Exercise: _____  ☐

· Relationships: _____  ☐

· Focus: _____  ☐

· _____  ☐

· _____  ☐

· _____  ☐

I'm *grateful* for: _____

_____

_____

| SLEEP | In bed | Devices off | Asleep by | Awake at | # sleep hours |
|-------|--------|-------------|-----------|----------|---------------|
| Plan  |        |             |           |          |               |
| Actual|        |             |           |          |               |

On a scale of 1-10, how well did you use your time?  _____

What was fun or went well? When did you feel most engaged & alive?

_____

_____

_____

_____

What did you learn? What do you wish you did *better* or *differently*?

_____

_____

_____

_____

Any funny, sad or difficult moments? _____

_____

_____

_____

_____

Write or draw *anything*:

# Plan for Tomorrow[7]

Date: Sunday _____

Three **Most Important** Things To Do:  *(do them ASAP)*          *Done*

1. _____  ☐

   _____

2. _____  ☐

   _____

3. _____  ☐

   _____

**Key goals & habits** for tomorrow:          *Done*

· Food: _____  ☐

· Drink: _____  ☐

· Exercise: _____  ☐

· Relationships: _____  ☐

· Focus: _____  ☐

· _____  ☐

· _____  ☐

· _____  ☐

I'm *grateful* for: _____

_____

_____

| SLEEP | In bed | Devices off | Asleep by | Awake at | # sleep hours |
|--------|--------|-------------|-----------|----------|---------------|
| Plan   |        |             |           |          |               |
| Actual |        |             |           |          |               |

On a scale of 1-10, how well did you use your time?     _____

What was fun or went well? When did you feel most engaged & alive?

_____

_____

_____

_____

What did you learn? What do you wish you did *better* or *differently*?

_____

_____

_____

_____

Any funny, sad or difficult moments? _____

_____

_____

_____

_____

Write or draw *anything*:

_____ _thru_ _____

Did you accomplish last week's **_Most Critical Thing_**?  ☐ No  ☐ Yes

Summarize what happened: _____

_____

_____

_____

_____

What did you do well? _____

_____

_____

What do you wish you did differently? _____

_____

_____

Were your _"I'm grateful for…"_ responses thoughtful & heartfelt?

☐ Not really   ☐ Somewhat   ☐ Mostly   ☐ Definitely

How well did you use your _time_? _(top-right, "Day in Review" pages)_

| Mon | Tues | Wed | Thurs | Fri | Sat | Sun | Total | Average |
|-----|------|-----|-------|-----|-----|-----|-------|---------|
|     |      |     |       |     |     |     |       |         |

Is your average _better, equal_ or _worse_ than the prior week? _____

Did you work on the *right things*, in the *right order*? If not, why?

_____

_____

_____

_____

Were you laser-*focused* or easily distracted? What were the worst *distractions* & time-wasters? How can you manage or avoid them?

_____

_____

_____

_____

Compare your *effort* last week to the very best you are capable of:

_____

_____

_____

_____

Was your overall *attitude* mostly positive and enthusiastic, or something else? How did that affect you?

_____

_____

_____

_____

And now some fun:    # Streaking!

Mark the circle for each item "done" on the corresponding day:

| # of incoming streak days | Mon | Tues | Wed | Thurs | Fri | Sat | Sun |
|---|---|---|---|---|---|---|---|
| Wrote in Journal | ○ | ○ | ○ | ○ | ○ | ○ | ○ |
| Important #1 | ○ | ○ | ○ | ○ | ○ | ○ | ○ |
| Important #2 | ○ | ○ | ○ | ○ | ○ | ○ | ○ |
| Important #3 | ○ | ○ | ○ | ○ | ○ | ○ | ○ |
| Food | ○ | ○ | ○ | ○ | ○ | ○ | ○ |
| Drink | ○ | ○ | ○ | ○ | ○ | ○ | ○ |
| Exercise | ○ | ○ | ○ | ○ | ○ | ○ | ○ |
| Relationships | ○ | ○ | ○ | ○ | ○ | ○ | ○ |
| Focus | ○ | ○ | ○ | ○ | ○ | ○ | ○ |
| (1st blank item) | ○ | ○ | ○ | ○ | ○ | ○ | ○ |
| (2nd blank item) | ○ | ○ | ○ | ○ | ○ | ○ | ○ |
| (3rd blank item) | ○ | ○ | ○ | ○ | ○ | ○ | ○ |

Every time you have at least 3 boxes in a row or all the boxes in a column checked, draw a vertical or horizontal line through them.

* Three days in a row of checked circles, even if some are from last week, means **YOU ARE <u>STREAKING!</u>**

* If every box in *one* entire row is checked, you are on a **POWER STREAK!** Awesome!

* If *every* box, in *every* row, is checked, you are on a **<u>MONSTER STREAK!</u>** Congratulations! You are Incredible!

Did you make meaningful progress towards your **long-term** goals last week? How can next week be better?

_____

_____

_____

How do you feel about your direction & progress for each item below? What changes should you make next week?

Food / Drink: _____

_____

_____

Exercise: _____

_____

_____

Relationships: _____

_____

_____

Focus: _____

_____

_____

Sleep: _____

*Enter your actual # of sleep hours from last week:*

| Sun | Mon | Tues | Wed | Thurs | Fri | Sat | Total | Average |
|-----|-----|------|-----|-------|-----|-----|-------|---------|
|     |     |      |     |       |     |     |       |         |

Notes, ideas, **and** how you feel about your direction & progress for **other things\*** you focused on last week:

---

---

---

---

---

---

---

---

---

---

---

---

---

---

---

---

---

\* *Such as work, school, personal finances, meditation, prayer, reading, learning, long-term goals, mental health, dental habits, volunteering, etc.*

## Plan for <u>Next</u> Week <sub>7</sub> _____ *thru* _____

What is the **Most Critical Thing** next week, over which you have at least *some* control? Why is it so important?

_____

_____

_____

With your *best* effort, is it *possible* for you to succeed?  ☐ No  ☐ Yes

What is the #1 thing *you* can do to ensure a successful outcome?

_____

_____

_____

What else must you do to prepare and execute most effectively? Be specific. Outline *when* and *how* you will do each of them.

_____

_____

_____

_____

_____

_____

_____

_____

What are you happy or excited about this week?

_____

_____

_____

What's likely to be difficult this week? How can you best handle it?

_____

_____

_____

Which of your relationships would benefit from some extra effort? Does anyone need your help? Consider taking action *this week.*

_____

_____

_____

What do you need to do during *the next seven days* to make meaningful progress towards your **long-term goals**?

_____

_____

_____

What *key goal or habit* do you want to focus on this week? How?

_____

_____

_____

## <u>7 Day Calendar + Notes</u>    *( schedule your priorities <u>*first*</u> )*

Monday _____   _____
          *(date)*

_____

_____

_____

_____

_____

Tuesday _____   _____
          *(date)*

_____

_____

_____

_____

_____

Wednesday _____   _____
          *(date)*

_____

_____

_____

_____

_____

Thursday _____ _____
*(date)*

_____

_____

_____

_____

Friday _____ _____
*(date)*

_____

_____

_____

_____

Saturday _____ _____
*(date)*

_____

_____

_____

_____

Sunday _____ _____
*(date)*

_____

_____

_____

_____

# Plan for Tomorrow[1]

Date: Monday _____

Three **Most Important** Things To Do:  *(do them ASAP)*  Done

1. _____ ☐

   _____

2. _____ ☐

   _____

3. _____ ☐

   _____

## Key goals & habits for tomorrow:  Done

· Food: _____ ☐

· Drink: _____ ☐

· Exercise: _____ ☐

· Relationships: _____ ☐

· Focus: _____ ☐

· _____ ☐

· _____ ☐

· _____ ☐

I'm *grateful* for: _____

_____

_____

| SLEEP | In bed | Devices off | Asleep by | Awake at | # sleep hours |
|---|---|---|---|---|---|
| Plan | | | | | |
| Actual | | | | | |

On a scale of 1-10, how well did you use your time?  _____

What was fun or went well?  When did you feel most engaged & alive?

_____

_____

_____

_____

What did you learn? What do you wish you did *better* or *differently*?

_____

_____

_____

_____

Any funny, sad or difficult moments?  _____

_____

_____

_____

_____

Write or draw *anything*:

# Plan for Tomorrow₂

Date: Tuesday _____

Three **Most Important** Things To Do:   *(do them ASAP)*     *Done*

1. _____   ☐

   _____

2. _____   ☐

   _____

3. _____   ☐

   _____

**Key goals & habits** for tomorrow:                          *Done*

· Food: _____   ☐

· Drink: _____   ☐

· Exercise: _____   ☐

· Relationships: _____   ☐

· Focus: _____   ☐

· _____   ☐

· _____   ☐

· _____   ☐

I'm *grateful* for: _____

_____

_____

| SLEEP | In bed | Devices off | Asleep by | Awake at | # sleep hours |
|---|---|---|---|---|---|
| Plan | | | | | |
| Actual | | | | | |

On a scale of 1-10, how well did you use your time? _____

What was fun or went well? When did you feel most engaged & alive?

_____

_____

_____

_____

What did you learn? What do you wish you did *better* or *differently*?

_____

_____

_____

_____

Any funny, sad or difficult moments? _____

_____

_____

_____

_____

Write or draw *anything*:

# Plan for Tomorrow₃

Date: Wednesday _____

Three **Most Important** Things To Do:  *(do them ASAP)*      *Done*

1. _____  ☐

    _____

2. _____  ☐

    _____

3. _____  ☐

    _____

**Key goals & habits** for tomorrow:      *Done*

· Food: _____  ☐

· Drink: _____  ☐

· Exercise: _____  ☐

· Relationships: _____  ☐

· Focus: _____  ☐

· _____  ☐

· _____  ☐

· _____  ☐

I'm *grateful* for: _____

_____

_____

| SLEEP | In bed | Devices off | Asleep by | Awake at | # sleep hours |
|-------|--------|-------------|-----------|----------|---------------|
| Plan |  |  |  |  |  |
| Actual |  |  |  |  |  |

On a scale of 1-10, how well did you use your time?           _____

What was fun or went well?  When did you feel most engaged & alive?

_____

_____

_____

_____

What did you learn? What do you wish you did *better* or *differently*?

_____

_____

_____

_____

Any funny, sad or difficult moments?  _____

_____

_____

_____

_____

Write or draw *anything*:

# Plan for Tomorrow[4]

Date: Thursday _____

Three **Most Important** Things To Do:  *(do them ASAP)*    *Done*

1. _____  ☐

_____

2. _____  ☐

_____

3. _____  ☐

_____

**Key goals & habits** for tomorrow:    *Done*

- Food: _____  ☐

- Drink: _____  ☐

- Exercise: _____  ☐

- Relationships: _____  ☐

- Focus: _____  ☐

- _____  ☐

- _____  ☐

- _____  ☐

I'm *grateful* for: _____

_____

_____

| SLEEP | In bed | Devices off | Asleep by | Awake at | # sleep hours |
|-------|--------|-------------|-----------|----------|---------------|
| Plan |  |  |  |  |  |
| Actual |  |  |  |  |  |

On a scale of 1-10, how well did you use your time?     _____

What was fun or went well? When did you feel most engaged & alive?

_____

_____

_____

_____

What did you learn? What do you wish you did *better* or *differently*?

_____

_____

_____

_____

Any funny, sad or difficult moments? _____

_____

_____

_____

_____

Write or draw *anything*:

# Plan for Tomorrow₅

Date: Friday _____

Three **Most Important** Things To Do: *(do them ASAP)*    *Done*

1. _____ ☐

    _____

2. _____ ☐

    _____

3. _____ ☐

    _____

**Key goals & habits** for tomorrow:    *Done*

· Food: _____ ☐

· Drink: _____ ☐

· Exercise: _____ ☐

· Relationships: _____ ☐

· Focus: _____ ☐

· _____ ☐

· _____ ☐

· _____ ☐

I'm *grateful* for: _____

_____

_____

| SLEEP | In bed | Devices off | Asleep by | Awake at | # sleep hours |
|-------|--------|-------------|-----------|----------|---------------|
| Plan  |        |             |           |          |               |
| Actual |       |             |           |          |               |

# Day in Review

On a scale of 1-10, how well did you use your time? _____

What was fun or went well? When did you feel most engaged & alive?

_____

_____

_____

_____

What did you learn? What do you wish you did *better* or *differently*?

_____

_____

_____

_____

Any funny, sad or difficult moments? _____

_____

_____

_____

_____

Write or draw *anything*:

# Plan for Tomorrow[6]

Date:  Saturday  _____

Three **Most Important** Things To Do:   *(do them ASAP)*          *Done*

1.  _____     ☐

   _____

2.  _____     ☐

   _____

3.  _____     ☐

   _____


**Key goals & habits** for tomorrow:                         *Done*

· Food: _____     ☐

· Drink: _____     ☐

· Exercise: _____     ☐

· Relationships: _____     ☐

· Focus: _____     ☐

· _____     ☐

· _____     ☐

· _____     ☐

I'm *grateful* for: _____

_____

_____

| SLEEP | In bed | Devices off | Asleep by | Awake at | # sleep hours |
|---|---|---|---|---|---|
| Plan | | | | | |
| Actual | | | | | |

On a scale of 1-10, how well did you use your time?        _____

What was fun or went well? When did you feel most engaged & alive?

_____

_____

_____

_____

What did you learn? What do you wish you did *better* or *differently*?

_____

_____

_____

_____

Any funny, sad or difficult moments? _____

_____

_____

_____

_____

Write or draw *anything*:

# Plan for Tomorrow[7]

Date: Sunday _____

Three **Most Important** Things To Do: *(do them ASAP)*     *Done*

1. _____ ☐

   _____

2. _____ ☐

   _____

3. _____ ☐

   _____

**Key goals & habits** for tomorrow:     *Done*

· Food: _____ ☐

· Drink: _____ ☐

· Exercise: _____ ☐

· Relationships: _____ ☐

· Focus: _____ ☐

· _____ ☐

· _____ ☐

· _____ ☐

I'm *grateful* for: _____

_____

_____

| SLEEP | In bed | Devices off | Asleep by | Awake at | # sleep hours |
|---|---|---|---|---|---|
| Plan | | | | | |
| Actual | | | | | |

On a scale of 1-10, how well did you use your time? _____

What was fun or went well? When did you feel most engaged & alive?

_____

_____

_____

_____

What did you learn? What do you wish you did *better* or *differently*?

_____

_____

_____

_____

Any funny, sad or difficult moments? _____

_____

_____

_____

_____

Write or draw *anything*:

## Last Week in Review _____ *thru* _____

Did you accomplish last week's **Most Critical Thing**?  ☐ No  ☐ Yes

Summarize what happened: _____

_____

_____

_____

_____

What did you do well? _____

_____

_____

_____

What do you wish you did differently? _____

_____

_____

_____

Were your *"I'm grateful for..."* responses thoughtful & heartfelt?

☐ Not really  ☐ Somewhat  ☐ Mostly  ☐ Definitely

How well did you use your *time*? *(top-right, "Day in Review" pages)*

| Mon | Tues | Wed | Thurs | Fri | Sat | Sun | Total | Average |
|-----|------|-----|-------|-----|-----|-----|-------|---------|
|     |      |     |       |     |     |     |       |         |

Is your average *better, equal* or *worse* than the prior week? _____

Did you work on the *right things*, in the *right order*? If not, why?

_____

_____

_____

_____

Were you laser-*focused* or easily distracted? What were the worst *distractions* & time-wasters? How can you manage or avoid them?

_____

_____

_____

_____

Compare your *effort* last week to the very best you are capable of:

_____

_____

_____

_____

Was your overall *attitude* mostly positive and enthusiastic, or something else? How did that affect you?

_____

_____

_____

_____

And now some fun:   **Streaking!**

Mark the circle for each item "done" on the corresponding day:

| # of incoming streak days | Mon | Tues | Wed | Thurs | Fri | Sat | Sun |
|---|---|---|---|---|---|---|---|
| Wrote in Journal | ○ | ○ | ○ | ○ | ○ | ○ | ○ |
| Important #1 | ○ | ○ | ○ | ○ | ○ | ○ | ○ |
| Important #2 | ○ | ○ | ○ | ○ | ○ | ○ | ○ |
| Important #3 | ○ | ○ | ○ | ○ | ○ | ○ | ○ |
| Food | ○ | ○ | ○ | ○ | ○ | ○ | ○ |
| Drink | ○ | ○ | ○ | ○ | ○ | ○ | ○ |
| Exercise | ○ | ○ | ○ | ○ | ○ | ○ | ○ |
| Relationships | ○ | ○ | ○ | ○ | ○ | ○ | ○ |
| Focus | ○ | ○ | ○ | ○ | ○ | ○ | ○ |
| (1st blank item) | ○ | ○ | ○ | ○ | ○ | ○ | ○ |
| (2nd blank item) | ○ | ○ | ○ | ○ | ○ | ○ | ○ |
| (3rd blank item) | ○ | ○ | ○ | ○ | ○ | ○ | ○ |

Every time you have at least 3 boxes in a row or all the boxes in a column checked, draw a vertical or horizontal line through them.

   * Three days in a row of checked circles, even if some are from last week, means **YOU ARE <u>STREAKING!</u>**

   * If every box in *one* entire row is checked, you are on a **POWER STREAK!** Awesome!

   * If *every* box, in *every* row, is checked, you are on a **MONSTER STREAK!** Congratulations! You are Incredible!

Did you make meaningful progress towards your **long-term** goals last week? How can next week be better?

_____

_____

_____

How do you feel about your direction & progress for each item below? What changes should you make next week?

Food / Drink: _____

_____

_____

Exercise: _____

_____

_____

Relationships: _____

_____

_____

Focus: _____

_____

_____

Sleep: _____

*Enter your actual # of sleep hours from last week:*

| Sun | Mon | Tues | Wed | Thurs | Fri | Sat | Total | Average |
|-----|-----|------|-----|-------|-----|-----|-------|---------|
|     |     |      |     |       |     |     |       |         |

Notes, ideas, **and** how you feel about your direction & progress for **other things*** you focused on last week:

_____

_____

_____

_____

_____

_____

_____

_____

_____

_____

_____

_____

_____

_____

_____

_____

_____

*Such as work, school, personal finances, meditation, prayer, reading, learning, long-term goals, mental health, dental habits, volunteering, etc.*

### Keep making progress!

You'll finish this journal in a few weeks.

Order your next one *today* at:

# streakersjournal.com

Use offer code *streaker* to save 15%

plus FREE shipping *(in the U.S.A.)*

# Plan for <u>Next</u> Week <sub>8</sub> _____ *thru* _____

What is the **Most Critical Thing** next week, over which you have at least *some* control? Why is it so important?

_____

_____

_____

With your *best* effort, is it *possible* for you to succeed? ☐ No ☐ Yes

What is the #1 thing *you* can do to ensure a successful outcome?

_____

_____

_____

What else must you do to prepare and execute most effectively? Be specific. Outline *when* and *how* you will do each of them.

_____

_____

_____

_____

_____

_____

_____

_____

_____

What are you happy or excited about this week?

_____

_____

_____

What's likely to be difficult this week? How can you best handle it?

_____

_____

_____

Is there anything regarding your or a loved one's health you've been putting off (e.g., doctor/dentist)? Consider doing it *this week.*

_____

_____

_____

What do you need to do during *the next seven days* to make meaningful progress towards your **long-term goals**?

_____

_____

_____

What *key goal or habit* do you want to focus on this week? How?

_____

_____

_____

## 7 Day Calendar + Notes        *( schedule your priorities **first** )*

Monday _____  _____
           *(date)*

_____

_____

_____

_____

_____

Tuesday _____  _____
            *(date)*

_____

_____

_____

_____

_____

Wednesday _____  _____
               *(date)*

_____

_____

_____

_____

_____

Thursday _____
*(date)*

_____

_____

_____

_____

_____

Friday _____
*(date)*

_____

_____

_____

_____

_____

Saturday _____
*(date)*

_____

_____

_____

_____

_____

Sunday _____
*(date)*

_____

_____

_____

_____

# Plan for Tomorrow[1]

Date: Monday _____

Three **Most Important** Things To Do:   *(do them ASAP)*                    *Done*

1. _____   ☐

   _____

2. _____   ☐

   _____

3. _____   ☐

   _____

**Key goals & habits** for tomorrow:                              *Done*

· Food: _____   ☐

· Drink: _____   ☐

· Exercise: _____   ☐

· Relationships: _____   ☐

· Focus: _____   ☐

· _____   ☐

· _____   ☐

· _____   ☐

I'm *grateful* for: _____

_____

_____

| SLEEP | In bed | Devices off | Asleep by | Awake at | # sleep hours |
|-------|--------|-------------|-----------|----------|---------------|
| Plan  |        |             |           |          |               |
| Actual |       |             |           |          |               |

On a scale of 1-10, how well did you use your time?  _____

What was fun or went well? When did you feel most engaged & alive?

_____

_____

_____

_____

What did you learn? What do you wish you did *better* or *differently*?

_____

_____

_____

_____

Any funny, sad or difficult moments? _____

_____

_____

_____

_____

Write or draw *anything*:

# Plan for Tomorrow₂

Date: Tuesday _____

Three **Most Important** Things To Do:  *(do them ASAP)*  *Done*

1. _____ ☐

_____

2. _____ ☐

_____

3. _____ ☐

_____

**Key goals & habits** for tomorrow:  *Done*

· Food: _____ ☐

· Drink: _____ ☐

· Exercise: _____ ☐

· Relationships: _____ ☐

· Focus: _____ ☐

· _____ ☐

· _____ ☐

· _____ ☐

I'm *grateful* for: _____

_____

_____

| SLEEP | In bed | Devices off | Asleep by | Awake at | # sleep hours |
|-------|--------|-------------|-----------|----------|---------------|
| Plan |  |  |  |  |  |
| Actual |  |  |  |  |  |

# Day in Review

On a scale of 1-10, how well did you use your time?  _____

What was fun or went well? When did you feel most engaged & alive?

_____

_____

_____

_____

What did you learn? What do you wish you did *better* or *differently*?

_____

_____

_____

_____

Any funny, sad or difficult moments? _____

_____

_____

_____

Write or draw *anything*:

# Plan for Tomorrow₃

Date: Wednesday _____

Three **Most Important** Things To Do:  *(do them ASAP)*  *Done*

1. _____  ☐

_____

2. _____  ☐

_____

3. _____  ☐

_____

**Key goals & habits** for tomorrow:  *Done*

· Food: _____  ☐

· Drink: _____  ☐

· Exercise: _____  ☐

· Relationships: _____  ☐

· Focus: _____  ☐

· _____  ☐

· _____  ☐

· _____  ☐

I'm *grateful* for: _____

_____

_____

| SLEEP | In bed | Devices off | Asleep by | Awake at | # sleep hours |
|-------|--------|-------------|-----------|----------|---------------|
| Plan | | | | | |
| Actual | | | | | |

On a scale of 1-10, how well did you use your time? _____

What was fun or went well? When did you feel most engaged & alive?

_____

_____

_____

_____

What did you learn? What do you wish you did _better_ or _differently_?

_____

_____

_____

_____

Any funny, sad or difficult moments? _____

_____

_____

_____

_____

Write or draw _anything_:

# Plan for Tomorrow₄

Date: Thursday _____

Three **Most Important** Things To Do:  *(do them ASAP)*     *Done*

1. _____ ☐

_____

2. _____ ☐

_____

3. _____ ☐

_____

**Key goals & habits** for tomorrow:     *Done*

· Food: _____ ☐

· Drink: _____ ☐

· Exercise: _____ ☐

· Relationships: _____ ☐

· Focus: _____ ☐

· _____ ☐

· _____ ☐

· _____ ☐

I'm *grateful* for: _____

_____

_____

| SLEEP | In bed | Devices off | Asleep by | Awake at | # sleep hours |
|-------|--------|-------------|-----------|----------|---------------|
| Plan  |        |             |           |          |               |
| Actual|        |             |           |          |               |

On a scale of 1-10, how well did you use your time?  _____

What was fun or went well? When did you feel most engaged & alive?

_____

_____

_____

_____

What did you learn? What do you wish you did _better_ or _differently_?

_____

_____

_____

_____

Any funny, sad or difficult moments?  _____

_____

_____

_____

_____

Write or draw _anything_:

# Plan for Tomorrow₅

Date: Friday _____

Three **Most Important** Things To Do:  *(do them ASAP)*      *Done*

1. _____  ☐

   _____

2. _____  ☐

   _____

3. _____  ☐

   _____

**Key goals & habits** for tomorrow:      *Done*

· Food: _____  ☐

· Drink: _____  ☐

· Exercise: _____  ☐

· Relationships: _____  ☐

· Focus: _____  ☐

· _____  ☐

· _____  ☐

· _____  ☐

I'm *grateful* for: _____

_____

_____

| SLEEP | In bed | Devices off | Asleep by | Awake at | # sleep hours |
|---|---|---|---|---|---|
| Plan | | | | | |
| Actual | | | | | |

On a scale of 1-10, how well did you use your time? _____

What was fun or went well?  When did you feel most engaged & alive?

_____

_____

_____

_____

What did you learn?  What do you wish you did *better* or *differently*?

_____

_____

_____

_____

Any funny, sad or difficult moments? _____

_____

_____

_____

_____

Write or draw *anything*:

# Plan for Tomorrow<sub>6</sub>

Date: Saturday _____

Three **Most Important** Things To Do: *(do them ASAP)*     *Done*

1. _____ ☐

   _____

2. _____ ☐

   _____

3. _____ ☐

   _____

**Key goals & habits** for tomorrow:     *Done*

· Food: _____ ☐

· Drink: _____ ☐

· Exercise: _____ ☐

· Relationships: _____ ☐

· Focus: _____ ☐

· _____ ☐

· _____ ☐

· _____ ☐

I'm *grateful* for: _____

_____

_____

| SLEEP | In bed | Devices off | Asleep by | Awake at | # sleep hours |
|---|---|---|---|---|---|
| Plan | | | | | |
| Actual | | | | | |

On a scale of 1-10, how well did you use your time? _____

What was fun or went well? When did you feel most engaged & alive?

_____

_____

_____

_____

What did you learn? What do you wish you did *better* or *differently*?

_____

_____

_____

_____

Any funny, sad or difficult moments? _____

_____

_____

_____

Write or draw *anything*:

# Plan for Tomorrow[7]

Date: Sunday _____

Three **Most Important** Things To Do:  *(do them ASAP)*  *Done*

1. _____ ☐

_____

2. _____ ☐

_____

3. _____ ☐

_____

## Key goals & habits for tomorrow:

*Done*

· Food: _____ ☐

· Drink: _____ ☐

· Exercise: _____ ☐

· Relationships: _____ ☐

· Focus: _____ ☐

· _____ ☐

· _____ ☐

· _____ ☐

I'm *grateful* for: _____

_____

_____

| SLEEP | In bed | Devices off | Asleep by | Awake at | # sleep hours |
|-------|--------|-------------|-----------|----------|---------------|
| Plan  |        |             |           |          |               |
| Actual|        |             |           |          |               |

On a scale of 1-10, how well did you use your time?     _____

What was fun or went well? When did you feel most engaged & alive?

_____

_____

_____

_____

What did you learn? What do you wish you did *better* or *differently*?

_____

_____

_____

_____

Any funny, sad or difficult moments? _____

_____

_____

_____

_____

Write or draw *anything*:

Did you accomplish last week's **_Most Critical Thing_**? ☐ No ☐ Yes

Summarize what happened: _____

_____

_____

_____

_____

What did you do well? _____

_____

_____

_____

What do you wish you did differently? _____

_____

_____

_____

Were your _"I'm grateful for..."_ responses thoughtful & heartfelt?

☐ Not really   ☐ Somewhat   ☐ Mostly   ☐ Definitely

How well did you use your _time_? _(top-right, "Day in Review" pages)_

| Mon | Tues | Wed | Thurs | Fri | Sat | Sun | Total | Average |
|-----|------|-----|-------|-----|-----|-----|-------|---------|
|     |      |     |       |     |     |     |       |         |

Is your average _better, equal_ or _worse_ than the prior week? _____

Did you work on the *right things*, in the *right order*? If not, why?

_____

_____

_____

_____

Were you laser-*focused* or easily distracted? What were the worst *distractions* & time-wasters? How can you manage or avoid them?

_____

_____

_____

_____

Compare your *effort* last week to the very best you are capable of:

_____

_____

_____

_____

Was your overall *attitude* mostly positive and enthusiastic, or something else? How did that affect you?

_____

_____

_____

_____

**And now some fun:** ## Streaking!

Mark the circle for each item "done" on the corresponding day:

| # of incoming streak days |

| | Mon | Tues | Wed | Thurs | Fri | Sat | Sun |
|---|---|---|---|---|---|---|---|
| Wrote in Journal | ○ | ○ | ○ | ○ | ○ | ○ | ○ |
| Important #1 | ○ | ○ | ○ | ○ | ○ | ○ | ○ |
| Important #2 | ○ | ○ | ○ | ○ | ○ | ○ | ○ |
| Important #3 | ○ | ○ | ○ | ○ | ○ | ○ | ○ |
| Food | ○ | ○ | ○ | ○ | ○ | ○ | ○ |
| Drink | ○ | ○ | ○ | ○ | ○ | ○ | ○ |
| Exercise | ○ | ○ | ○ | ○ | ○ | ○ | ○ |
| Relationships | ○ | ○ | ○ | ○ | ○ | ○ | ○ |
| Focus | ○ | ○ | ○ | ○ | ○ | ○ | ○ |
| *(1st blank item)* | ○ | ○ | ○ | ○ | ○ | ○ | ○ |
| *(2nd blank item)* | ○ | ○ | ○ | ○ | ○ | ○ | ○ |
| *(3rd blank item)* | ○ | ○ | ○ | ○ | ○ | ○ | ○ |

Every time you have at least 3 boxes in a row or all the boxes in a column checked, draw a vertical or horizontal line through them.

* Three days in a row of checked circles, even if some are from last week, means **YOU ARE <u>STREAKING</u>!**

* If every box in *one* entire row is checked, you are on a **POWER STREAK!** Awesome!

* If *every* box, in *every* row, is checked, you are on a **<u>MONSTER</u> STREAK!** Congratulations! You are Incredible!

Did you make meaningful progress towards your **long-term** goals last week? How can next week be better?

_____

_____

_____

How do you feel about your direction & progress for each item below? What changes should you make next week?

Food/Drink: _____

_____

_____

Exercise: _____

_____

_____

Relationships: _____

_____

_____

Focus: _____

_____

_____

Sleep: _____

*Enter your actual # of sleep hours from last week:*

| Sun | Mon | Tues | Wed | Thurs | Fri | Sat | Total | Average |
|-----|-----|------|-----|-------|-----|-----|-------|---------|
|     |     |      |     |       |     |     |       |         |

Notes, ideas, **and** how you feel about your direction & progress for **other things**\* you focused on last week:

_____

_____

_____

_____

_____

_____

_____

_____

_____

_____

_____

_____

_____

_____

_____

_____

_____

_____

*\* Such as work, school, personal finances, meditation, prayer, reading, learning, long-term goals, mental health, dental habits, volunteering, etc.*

# Plan for **Next** Week <sub>9</sub> _____ *thru* _____

What is the **Most Critical Thing** next week, over which you have at least *some* control? Why is it so important?

_____

_____

_____

With your *best* effort, is it *possible* for you to succeed?  ☐ No  ☐ Yes

What is the #1 thing *you* can do to ensure a successful outcome?

_____

_____

_____

What else must you do to prepare and execute most effectively? Be specific. Outline *when* and *how* you will do each of them.

_____

_____

_____

_____

_____

_____

_____

_____

_____

What are you happy or excited about this week?

_____

_____

_____

What's likely to be difficult this week? How can you best handle it?

_____

_____

_____

Without spending any money, what could you do *for yourself* this week that would be fun, relaxing, enjoyable or interesting?

_____

_____

_____

What do you need to do during *the next seven days* to make meaningful progress towards your **long-term goals**?

_____

_____

_____

What *key goal or habit* do you want to focus on this week? How?

_____

_____

_____

## 7 Day Calendar + Notes     *( schedule your priorities **first** )*

Monday _____ _____
*(date)*

_____

_____

_____

_____

_____

Tuesday _____ _____
*(date)*

_____

_____

_____

_____

_____

Wednesday _____ _____
*(date)*

_____

_____

_____

_____

_____

Thursday _____ _____
*(date)*

_____

_____

_____

_____

Friday _____ _____
*(date)*

_____

_____

_____

_____

Saturday _____ _____
*(date)*

_____

_____

_____

_____

Sunday _____ _____
*(date)*

_____

_____

_____

# Plan for Tomorrow[1]

Date: Monday _____

Three **Most Important** Things To Do:  *(do them ASAP)*    *Done*

1. _____  ☐

   _____

2. _____  ☐

   _____

3. _____  ☐

   _____

**Key goals & habits** for tomorrow:    *Done*

- Food: _____  ☐

- Drink: _____  ☐

- Exercise: _____  ☐

- Relationships: _____  ☐

- Focus: _____  ☐

- _____  ☐

- _____  ☐

- _____  ☐

I'm *grateful* for: _____

_____

_____

| SLEEP | In bed | Devices off | Asleep by | Awake at | # sleep hours |
|-------|--------|-------------|-----------|----------|---------------|
| Plan   |        |             |           |          |               |
| Actual |        |             |           |          |               |

On a scale of 1-10, how well did you use your time?       _____

What was fun or went well?  When did you feel most engaged & alive?

_____

_____

_____

_____

What did you learn? What do you wish you did *better* or *differently*?

_____

_____

_____

_____

Any funny, sad or difficult moments?  _____

_____

_____

_____

_____

Write or draw *anything*:

# Plan for Tomorrow₂

Date: Tuesday _____

Three **Most Important** Things To Do:   *(do them ASAP)*                Done

1. _____  ☐

   _____

2. _____  ☐

   _____

3. _____  ☐

   _____

**Key goals & habits** for tomorrow:                                       *Done*

· Food: _____  ☐

· Drink: _____  ☐

· Exercise: _____  ☐

· Relationships: _____  ☐

· Focus: _____  ☐

· _____  ☐

· _____  ☐

· _____  ☐

I'm *grateful* for: _____

_____

_____

| SLEEP | In bed | Devices off | Asleep by | Awake at | # sleep hours |
|-------|--------|-------------|-----------|----------|---------------|
| Plan  |        |             |           |          |               |
| Actual|        |             |           |          |               |

# Day in Review

On a scale of 1-10, how well did you use your time? _____

What was fun or went well? When did you feel most engaged & alive?

_____

_____

_____

_____

What did you learn? What do you wish you did *better* or *differently*?

_____

_____

_____

_____

Any funny, sad or difficult moments? _____

_____

_____

_____

_____

Write or draw *anything*:

# Plan for Tomorrow₃

Date: Wednesday _____

Three **Most Important** Things To Do:   *(do them ASAP)*                Done

1. _____  ☐

   _____

2. _____  ☐

   _____

3. _____  ☐

   _____

**Key goals & habits** for tomorrow:                Done

· Food: _____  ☐

· Drink: _____  ☐

· Exercise: _____  ☐

· Relationships: _____  ☐

· Focus: _____  ☐

· _____  ☐

· _____  ☐

· _____  ☐

I'm *grateful* for: _____

_____

_____

| SLEEP | In bed | Devices off | Asleep by | Awake at | # sleep hours |
|-------|--------|-------------|-----------|----------|---------------|
| Plan | | | | | |
| Actual | | | | | |

# Day in Review

On a scale of 1-10, how well did you use your time?  _____

What was fun or went well?  When did you feel most engaged & alive?

_____

_____

_____

_____

What did you learn?  What do you wish you did *better* or *differently*?

_____

_____

_____

_____

Any funny, sad or difficult moments?  _____

_____

_____

_____

_____

Write or draw *anything*:

# Plan for Tomorrow[4]

Date: Thursday _____

Three **Most Important** Things To Do:   *(do them ASAP)*    *Done*

1. _____  ☐

   _____

2. _____  ☐

   _____

3. _____  ☐

   _____

**Key goals & habits** for tomorrow:    *Done*

· Food: _____  ☐

· Drink: _____  ☐

· Exercise: _____  ☐

· Relationships: _____  ☐

· Focus: _____  ☐

· _____  ☐

· _____  ☐

· _____  ☐

I'm *grateful* for: _____

_____

_____

| SLEEP | In bed | Devices off | Asleep by | Awake at | # sleep hours |
|-------|--------|-------------|-----------|----------|---------------|
| Plan  |        |             |           |          |               |
| Actual |       |             |           |          |               |

On a scale of 1-10, how well did you use your time? _____

What was fun or went well? When did you feel most engaged & alive?

_____

_____

_____

_____

What did you learn? What do you wish you did *better* or *differently*?

_____

_____

_____

Any funny, sad or difficult moments? _____

_____

_____

_____

Write or draw *anything*:

# Plan for Tomorrow₅

Date: Friday _____

Three **Most Important** Things To Do: *(do them ASAP)*        *Done*

1. _____ ☐

_____

2. _____ ☐

_____

3. _____ ☐

_____

**Key goals & habits** for tomorrow:        *Done*

· Food: _____ ☐

· Drink: _____ ☐

· Exercise: _____ ☐

· Relationships: _____ ☐

· Focus: _____ ☐

· _____ ☐

· _____ ☐

· _____ ☐

I'm *grateful* for: _____

_____

_____

| SLEEP | In bed | Devices off | Asleep by | Awake at | # sleep hours |
|---|---|---|---|---|---|
| Plan | | | | | |
| Actual | | | | | |

On a scale of 1-10, how well did you use your time?   _____

What was fun or went well? When did you feel most engaged & alive?

_____

_____

_____

_____

What did you learn? What do you wish you did *better* or *differently*?

_____

_____

_____

_____

Any funny, sad or difficult moments?  _____

_____

_____

_____

_____

Write or draw *anything*:

# Plan for Tomorrow[6]

Date: Saturday _____

Three **Most Important** Things To Do:   *(do them ASAP)*     *Done*

1. _____   ☐

   _____

2. _____   ☐

   _____

3. _____   ☐

   _____

**Key goals & habits** for tomorrow:                    *Done*

· Food: _____   ☐

· Drink: _____   ☐

· Exercise: _____   ☐

· Relationships: _____   ☐

· Focus: _____   ☐

· _____   ☐

· _____   ☐

· _____   ☐

I'm *grateful* for: _____

_____

_____

| SLEEP | In bed | Devices off | Asleep by | Awake at | # sleep hours |
|---|---|---|---|---|---|
| Plan | | | | | |
| Actual | | | | | |

On a scale of 1-10, how well did you use your time?    _____

What was fun or went well? When did you feel most engaged & alive?

_____

_____

_____

_____

What did you learn? What do you wish you did *better* or *differently*?

_____

_____

_____

_____

Any funny, sad or difficult moments? _____

_____

_____

_____

_____

Write or draw *anything*:

# Plan for Tomorrow[7]

Date: Sunday _____

Three **Most Important** Things To Do:  *(do them ASAP)*    *Done*

1. _____ ☐

   _____

2. _____ ☐

   _____

3. _____ ☐

   _____

**Key goals & habits** for tomorrow:    *Done*

· Food: _____ ☐

· Drink: _____ ☐

· Exercise: _____ ☐

· Relationships: _____ ☐

· Focus: _____ ☐

· _____ ☐

· _____ ☐

· _____ ☐

I'm *grateful* for: _____

_____

_____

| SLEEP | In bed | Devices off | Asleep by | Awake at | # sleep hours |
|---|---|---|---|---|---|
| Plan | | | | | |
| Actual | | | | | |

On a scale of 1-10, how well did you use your time? _____

What was fun or went well? When did you feel most engaged & alive?

_____

_____

_____

_____

What did you learn? What do you wish you did _better_ or _differently_?

_____

_____

_____

_____

Any funny, sad or difficult moments? _____

_____

_____

_____

Write or draw _anything_:

Did you accomplish last week's **Most Critical Thing**? ☐ No ☐ Yes

Summarize what happened: _____

_____

_____

_____

_____

What did you do well? _____

_____

_____

_____

What do you wish you did differently? _____

_____

_____

_____

Were your *"I'm grateful for..."* responses thoughtful & heartfelt?

☐ Not really    ☐ Somewhat    ☐ Mostly    ☐ Definitely

How well did you use your *time*? *(top-right, "Day in Review" pages)*

| Mon | Tues | Wed | Thurs | Fri | Sat | Sun | Total | Average |
|-----|------|-----|-------|-----|-----|-----|-------|---------|
|     |      |     |       |     |     |     |       |         |

Is your average *better, equal* or *worse* than the prior week? _____

Did you work on the *right things*, in the *right order*? If not, why?

_____

_____

_____

_____

Were you laser-*focused* or easily distracted? What were the worst *distractions* & time-wasters? How can you manage or avoid them?

_____

_____

_____

_____

Compare your *effort* last week to the very best you are capable of:

_____

_____

_____

_____

Was your overall *attitude* mostly positive and enthusiastic, or something else? How did that affect you?

_____

_____

_____

_____

And now some fun:     # Streaking!

Mark the circle for each item "done" on the corresponding day:

| # of incoming streak days | Mon | Tues | Wed | Thurs | Fri | Sat | Sun |
|---|---|---|---|---|---|---|---|
| Wrote in Journal | ○ | ○ | ○ | ○ | ○ | ○ | ○ |
| Important #1 | ○ | ○ | ○ | ○ | ○ | ○ | ○ |
| Important #2 | ○ | ○ | ○ | ○ | ○ | ○ | ○ |
| Important #3 | ○ | ○ | ○ | ○ | ○ | ○ | ○ |
| Food | ○ | ○ | ○ | ○ | ○ | ○ | ○ |
| Drink | ○ | ○ | ○ | ○ | ○ | ○ | ○ |
| Exercise | ○ | ○ | ○ | ○ | ○ | ○ | ○ |
| Relationships | ○ | ○ | ○ | ○ | ○ | ○ | ○ |
| Focus | ○ | ○ | ○ | ○ | ○ | ○ | ○ |
| (1st blank item) | ○ | ○ | ○ | ○ | ○ | ○ | ○ |
| (2nd blank item) | ○ | ○ | ○ | ○ | ○ | ○ | ○ |
| (3rd blank item) | ○ | ○ | ○ | ○ | ○ | ○ | ○ |

Every time you have at least 3 boxes in a row or all the boxes in a column checked, draw a vertical or horizontal line through them.

* Three days in a row of checked circles, even if some are from last week, means **YOU ARE <u>STREAKING!</u>**

* If every box in *one* entire row is checked, you are on a **POWER STREAK!** Awesome!

* If *every* box, in *every* row, is checked, you are on a **<u>MONSTER STREAK!</u>** Congratulations! You are Incredible!

Did you make meaningful progress towards your **long-term** goals last week? How can next week be better?

_____

_____

_____

How do you feel about your direction & progress for each item below? What changes should you make next week?

Food/Drink: _____

_____

_____

Exercise: _____

_____

_____

Relationships: _____

_____

_____

Focus: _____

_____

_____

Sleep: _____

*Enter your actual # of sleep hours from last week:*

| Sun | Mon | Tues | Wed | Thurs | Fri | Sat | Total | Average |
|-----|-----|------|-----|-------|-----|-----|-------|---------|
|     |     |      |     |       |     |     |       |         |

Notes, ideas, **and** how you feel about your direction & progress for **other things*** you focused on last week:

_____

_____

_____

_____

_____

_____

_____

_____

_____

_____

_____

_____

_____

_____

_____

_____

_____

*\* Such as work, school, personal finances, meditation, prayer, reading, learning, long-term goals, mental health, dental habits, volunteering, etc.*

## 9 Week Review

Nine weeks. It's not an especially long period of time, but it's long enough to have developed or changed habits and made real progress in your health, relationships, and much more.

Imagine you're writing a **short** letter to a trusted friend, updating them on what's happened in your life over the past nine weeks.

**Part 1 -** Briefly explain your situation when you first *started* this journal. What was going well and what wasn't? What did you hope to work on and accomplish? Why?

_____

_____

_____

_____

_____

_____

_____

_____

_____

_____

_____

_____

_____

**Part 2 -** What happened along the way? Were there any major personal or news events? Did you try or learn something new? Any important failures or achievements?

**Part 3 -** What's different about you & your life versus 9 weeks ago?

_____

_____

_____

_____

_____

_____

What have you learned over the last 9 weeks?

_____

_____

_____

_____

When did you feel most alive & engaged in what you were doing? Be specific about what it was + the circumstances surrounding it.

_____

_____

_____

_____

*What you wrote above might give some clues about things to build into your life (career, hobby, etc.). Learn more via the A+ book, "Designing Your Life."*

# 9 Week Review - Streaking!

Mark the circle for each item "done" on the corresponding week:

| | Check each item that was done *every* day of the corresponding week | | | | | | | | | *longest streak (days)* |
|---|---|---|---|---|---|---|---|---|---|---|
| week → | 1 | 2 | 3 | 4 | 5 | 6 | 7 | 8 | 9 | |
| Wrote in Journal | ○ | ○ | ○ | ○ | ○ | ○ | ○ | ○ | ○ | |
| Important #1 | ○ | ○ | ○ | ○ | ○ | ○ | ○ | ○ | ○ | |
| Important #2 | ○ | ○ | ○ | ○ | ○ | ○ | ○ | ○ | ○ | |
| Important #3 | ○ | ○ | ○ | ○ | ○ | ○ | ○ | ○ | ○ | |
| Food | ○ | ○ | ○ | ○ | ○ | ○ | ○ | ○ | ○ | |
| Drink | ○ | ○ | ○ | ○ | ○ | ○ | ○ | ○ | ○ | |
| Exercise | ○ | ○ | ○ | ○ | ○ | ○ | ○ | ○ | ○ | |
| Relationships | ○ | ○ | ○ | ○ | ○ | ○ | ○ | ○ | ○ | |
| Focus | ○ | ○ | ○ | ○ | ○ | ○ | ○ | ○ | ○ | |
| (1st blank item) | ○ | ○ | ○ | ○ | ○ | ○ | ○ | ○ | ○ | |
| (2nd blank item) | ○ | ○ | ○ | ○ | ○ | ○ | ○ | ○ | ○ | |
| (3rd blank item) | ○ | ○ | ○ | ○ | ○ | ○ | ○ | ○ | ○ | |

Describe your sleep habits & results over the last 9 weeks?

_____

_____

_____

_____

Describe your effort and progress on the "key goals & habits" below. What worked well? What will you change next time?

Food: _____

_____

_____

_____

Drink: _____

_____

_____

_____

Exercise: _____

_____

_____

_____

Relationships: _____

_____

_____

_____

Focus: _____

_____

_____

_____

Describe your progress towards your **long-term goals** (p. 25). Has your enthusiasm or certainty about them changed?

_____

_____

_____

_____

_____

_____

_____

_____

_____

Describe your progress towards your **9-week goals** (p. 28).

_____

_____

_____

_____

_____

_____

_____

_____

How well did you do at staying **focused** and avoiding distractions? What strategies were most effective? Which did not work?

_____

_____

_____

_____

_____

What are you most proud of from the last 9 weeks? Why?

_____

_____

_____

_____

_____

What do you wish you did differently over the last 9 weeks? Why?

_____

_____

_____

_____

_____

_____

# Blank Pages *(write or draw anything)*

# Keep Making Progress!

Order your next journal *today* at:

# streakersjournal.com

Use offer code **streaker** to save 15%

plus FREE shipping *(in the U.S.A.)*

*Thank you. It's been a privilege to be part of your life.*

Made in the USA
Columbia, SC
16 August 2019